MAKESHIFT FIELDS

Chasing Baseball Across Ireland, Scotland, England, and Wales

DALE JACOBS

INVISIBLE PUBLISHING
Halifax | Fredericton | Picton

Library and Archives Canada Cataloguing in Publication

Title: Makeshift fields : chasing baseball across Ireland, Scotland, England, and Wales / Dale Jacobs.
Names: Jacobs, Dale, 1966- author.
Identifiers: Canadiana 20240501756 | ISBN 9781778430619 (softcover)
Subjects: LCSH: Baseball—Ireland. | LCSH: Baseball—Scotland. | LCSH: Baseball—England. | LCSH: Baseball—Wales.
Classification: LCC GV863.467.A1 J33 2025 | DDC 796.3570941—dc23

Edited by Norm Nehmetallah and Gabriel E. Fidler
Cover design by Megan Fildes
Typeset in Laurentian with thanks to type designer Rod McDonald

Invisible Publishing is committed to protecting our natural environment. As part of our efforts, both the cover and interior of this book are printed on acid-free 100% post-consumer recycled fibres.

Printed and bound in Canada.

Invisible Publishing | Halifax, Fredericton, and Picton
www.invisiblepublishing.com

Published with the generous assistance of the Canada Council for the Arts, the Ontario Arts Council, and the Government of Canada.

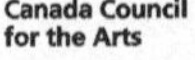

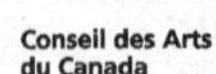

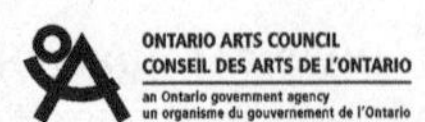

In sport players are the real storytellers, the sportswriters just translate the stories into words.

—TADHG COAKLEY, *THE GAME*

PRELUDE

"There's baseball in Ireland?"

It was a question I heard often in the days leading up to the trip. In fact, I heard this question every time I told someone about what I would be doing for seven weeks away from my home in Windsor, Ontario in the summer of 2023. As I explained that I would be starting in Ireland, but would then move on to Scotland, England, and Wales, it was clear that in their question, Ireland stood in for all of these places that we, in North America, do not associate with baseball. Sometimes they would politely listen as I described the arc of the trip, clearly more interested in the cities themselves than the prospect of baseball being played there. But other times, there would be a gleam of recognition, an excitement at the possibility of seeing baseball anew by not only moving beyond the major leagues, but by moving completely outside the context of North America and into a place about which people ask, "There's baseball there?"

I have spent a lot of time thinking about how baseball is played and what baseball means outside of the major leagues, especially within 100 miles of my house. In the summer of 2018, I watched, with my wife and co-author Heidi Jacobs, fifty games over one summer in that geographic range of our home. We saw games from high school to college to various levels of amateur ball, from the affiliated and unaffiliated minor leagues to the majors. We even watched baseball played under the rules of 1865. Based on that wonderful summer of baseball, we then wrote a two-voiced account of our experiences in what would become

100 Miles of Baseball (Biblioasis, 2021). That experience changed my relationship with the game by teaching me to slow down, to take in the big and the small details, to be less concerned with the score and more concerned with baseball itself, to see the beauty in the game when stepping away from watching only the best players on the planet. Through writing *100 Miles of Baseball*, I was also able to spend time thinking about my late father and what baseball meant to him throughout his life. Watching baseball in that way helped me, finally, to understand him better. When I finished writing about that summer, I thought I had said what I needed to say about the game. I could go back to being a civilian, albeit with a changed relationship to the sport that focused more on baseball writ large than on the results of any particular game. It turns out, though, that in terms of writing, baseball was not yet done with me.

The path that led to that discovery began with a tentative pursuit of basketball, a sport I was also attempting to understand better. At the same time, I was thinking about Ireland, reading contemporary Irish fiction for my coming graduate seminar, and plotting another trip back once we felt comfortable enough, post-COVID, to travel internationally. I wanted to see our friends in County Mayo, haunt the bookstores in Dublin, and sit with a pint and a book in Grogan's. And with a sabbatical approaching the following year, I was searching for a project, my subconscious constantly sifting through possibilities as I read and wrote and watched and walked. One day, as I walked the final block home, I was suddenly struck by the idea that I should see if there was professional basketball in Ireland. When I got home, I walked straight to my office, sat down at the computer, and searched *basketball Ireland*. At least, that's what I intended to do, but what I actually typed was *baseball Ireland*. Freudian slip? Muscle memory kicking in? A subtle nudge from the baseball gods? Whatever the reason, I was now staring at search results that started with *Baseball Ireland*, with subheadings that included *National Teams*, *Fixtures*, *Club Locator*, and *Teams*. Just below, in the *People also ask* section was the question, *Is there baseball in Ireland?* It was a question I hadn't even thought to ask.

Over the next hours and days, I spent a lot of time searching for baseball in other places where I had not expected to find it, blinkered as I was, not only by my location on the border between Canada and the United States, but also by years of watching major league baseball. I knew there were players in both the American and National leagues from Puerto Rico, Cuba, Japan, the Dominican Republic, Venezuela, South Korea, Mexico, Panama, Curaçao, and Colombia. I had also started to become aware of players from places such as Australia and Germany, countries that I soon discovered had their own professional leagues—the Australian Baseball League and the Bundesliga. But across Europe—from Italy to France to Spain to Czechia to the Netherlands to Norway to Poland to Great Britain and everywhere in between—there was baseball in a variety of professional and amateur leagues. The idea that baseball existed in all of these places and that there were people there who were passionate about the game was thrilling to me. The idea of chasing baseball to new—and, to me, unexpected—places was starting to get under my skin.

Through all my hours of going down the rabbit hole of baseball in Europe and through the evolution of an idea for a writing project about it, I kept coming back to Ireland, a country and a culture with which I had more than a passing familiarity. Should I focus on baseball in Ireland alone? Ireland and two or three countries on the continent? The permutations were at times overwhelming, and it wasn't until I sat down one evening and delved more fully into what baseball in Great Britain entailed that the project began to come into focus. It is—and should always have been—such an obvious approach, but it wasn't until I began to think of baseball in Scotland, Wales, and England, rather than baseball in Great Britain, that something clicked. In all of these countries, as in Ireland, there was no professional baseball within a landscape so heavily dominated by other sports. Hurling, camogie, Gaelic football, and rugby occupy most of the country's athletic imagination in Ireland, while football and rugby hold sway in Scotland, England, and Wales, as well as cricket in England. Baseball in these countries is, in every sense of the word, grassroots, a form of baseball I found increasingly appealing and from which I sensed I could most learn about the game. However, as I read, I also was coming to the understanding that baseball looked different in each of these places and that the local contexts shaped the game and the way people experienced it. As well, from a purely logistical perspective, the proximity of these locations to each other would make a summer baseball trip possible. Finally, much to my chagrin, I cannot speak any language other than English, a definite hindrance in trying to chase baseball in some parts of Europe. The general outlines of the project, and of the trip in support of it, were beginning to take shape.

As I began to plan the trip, I was immediately faced with the fact that all of the games were played on the weekends; no midweek games meant that the trip would have to be done over a longer time frame than I initially anticipated. I needed to see as many games as I could, but I realized early on that what was particularly important was that I have the opportunity to talk to the people involved with the game.

Why not choose specific clubs and spend a week shadowing each of them, not only attending a game, but attending practice (what I soon came to know as "training") as well? Five clubs in five weeks. That was the plan. Straightforward enough, I thought. That is, until I saw the schedules and began to try to assemble a route and timetable. No games on Father's Day. Several leagues suspending play for the London Series between the St. Louis Cardinals and the Chicago Cubs—only the second time Major League Baseball had played a regular season series in Europe. Bye weeks. Away games. My notebook had pages of possible itineraries, complete with circles and arrows and a set of notations that was more complicated than a scorecard for a Little League game. And then I got word of the British Baseball Federation Summer Cup at Farnham Park, Slough (west of London), to be held the second last weekend of July. So I started again, making sure that I could visit all of the clubs while still making it to Slough. Five clubs became seven clubs. Five weeks became seven weeks. The trip felt like it was spiralling out of control.

But eventually a workable itinerary began to emerge and I came to terms with the notion of being on the road for seven weeks. Thankfully, Heidi would be along for the ride, pursuing her own research, while I chased baseball across an array of cities. The complex logistics of scheduling meant that the trip would start in Dublin, a fitting place to begin, both because the discovery of baseball in Ireland had been the catalyst for this whole mad pursuit and because the Greystones Mariners (or "Mariners Baseball—Ireland"), who play their games in one of Dublin's south suburbs, was the first club I contacted. Through them, I discovered that there was a connection between Windsor, Ontario, where I live, and baseball in Ireland in the persons of Brendan

Power and Michael-Anthony Ferrato, who were both from Windsor but played for the Mariners and the Irish National Team at various times over the past ten years. Brendan lived in London, coaching and playing for the London Mets, but Mike was now a doctor in Windsor. Windsor being Windsor, it turned out that friends of ours were his patients. I took this small bit of happenstance as a positive sign. We arranged to meet for lunch on the only day that our schedules lined up: St. Patrick's Day.

As we sat and talked, the outlines of Mike's baseball career came into focus, and I began to see the echoes of so many people I knew in the amateur scene in Windsor and Essex County. Coming up with the Tecumseh Thunder Junior team before moving on to the Senior squad. Playing with the club team at the University of Windsor. Continuing to play even now with the Windsor Athletics. Not yet sliding into slo-pitch. Wanting to hold on for a few more years. Baseball was clearly part of his identity, a central feature of who he was that he did not want to give up. But it was as he began to tell me about playing in Ireland that the story changed to something beyond what was familiar to me, both in the details and the tenor of his voice. He was eligible to play for the Irish National Baseball Team by virtue of the fact that his mother had been born in Limerick, and he was offered a spot when the team was in need of a catcher for a tournament. Through that connection, he spent time playing not only for the National Team, but also off and on for the Mariners, a connection that persists, as he continues to travel to play in the occasional tournament. As he spoke, he mentioned several times how the boys were "great *craic*, as they say," a gleam in his eye underscoring his feelings about baseball in Ireland. It was Mike who told me the first of the many stories I would hear about Jaime Cuevas, a legendary player in Irish baseball who may or may not have played in the Mexican League. It was also Mike who advised me to seek out Sean Mitchell, "the man behind much baseball in Ireland." The stories he told—and the manner of their telling—would stay with me as I began the transition from thinking about baseball here to thinking about baseball there.

Not long after that lunch, the various league schedules were finalized and the itinerary at last fell into place. Dublin would be the base for the first week, but my activities there would extend well beyond Mariners' games and training and include time with the Ashbourne club; at least one visit to Strike Zone, the Irish Baseball Indoor Training Centre; and talks with Jason Wiebe and others at Baseball Ireland. From Dublin, we would make our way to Cork so that I could attend a training session of the new Renegades club, a team whose road games I would see both before and after my visit to Cork. Then I would head back to Dublin for a weekend of games to begin July before flying across the Irish Sea to Aberdeen for a few days. There I would attend a training session with the Granite City Oilers before taking the train to Edinburgh for midweek training and a weekend game, as well as conversations with people at Baseball Scotland. Dundee would be the next stop for just over a week that would include a Tayport Breakers' training session and game. Then a flight from Dundee to Slough via nearby Heathrow for the BBF Summer Cup, followed by a week in Cardiff that would include training and a game with the Cardiff Merlins. Finally, we would take the train to Leicester for a week that would include training and game time with both the Leicester Diamonds—the only women's team I would see on the trip—and the Leicester Blue Sox. From there, we would fly home. Fifty-two days on the road.

Fifty-two days of chasing baseball across four countries. Equal parts daunting and exciting.

And, of course, unpredictable. Not only were the details of the trip subject to the vagaries of the weather, a truth I had come up against often enough in trying to watch baseball in Ontario and Michigan in April and May, but this would also very much be grassroots baseball, where little is set in stone and where schedules are sometimes more like suggestions. As the date of departure drew closer, I had a general sense of the parameters of what I was doing, but little idea of what exactly I might find. I hoped to establish a picture of the games, the places they are played, the people who are involved, and the place it occupies in the lives of the players, coaches, umpires, and spectators. In visiting all of these locales, I hoped, above all, to understand: why baseball? In those observations and conversations, I hoped to learn something larger about baseball itself. But in doing so, I was going to need to be flexible, to roll with local events and circumstances, and to be open to whatever possibilities presented themselves if I was going to follow baseball wherever it would lead me.

DUBLIN

It's an American sport, but it's going to be Irish baseball.

—FRANK ANDREWS, DEVELOPMENT COACH, BASEBALL IRELAND

MONDAY, JUNE 19, 2023

I'm in the back of a cab, headed down the M-50 on the way from the Dublin airport to our apartment in Glasnevin. Ten a.m. and I haven't slept now for nearly twenty-four hours. The motorway yields to city streets, industrial estates, parks, blocks of flats, all in a different configuration than I've seen on other trips to Dublin. Where we're staying and where baseball is played are not the Dublin I know from previous trips—St. Stephen's Green, Trinity, the Abbey Theatre, Grogan's and the Palace Bar, Grafton Street, Hodges Figgis and Books Upstairs, Phoenix Park, Kilmainham—a Dublin that mainly encompasses city centre, circumscribed by the Liffey and the Grand Canal. As I began to plan, my mental map of Dublin quickly expanded: to Finglas and Ashbourne in the north, to Shankill in the south, and to Corkagh Park in the southwest. As we slide past a giant Tesco, I take out my phone to check the map. Just a few blocks more until I can finally get some sleep.

The cab driver lets us off in front of what will be our home for the next week, a building that looks almost exactly like the other two that flank it on the Finglas Road.

I pull up the instructions from our host, find the lockbox, retrieve the key, and begin to walk toward the main doors. The buildings surround a courtyard of grass and cement, a place where I imagine kids play on warm summer evenings. As I look towards the entrance, though, I see a large sign, white letters on a bright red background, that says, *NO BALL GAMES PERMITTED*. I snap a photo, knowing that I will post it to Instagram with a flip comment about how I hope this does not bode ill. But in my sleep-deprived state, part of me really does wonder about that sign, about what I'm doing in the north of Dublin, about why I'm searching for baseball here.

We force ourselves to get up in the mid-afternoon so that we will be able to sleep tonight and so that, hopefully, our bodies will be able to adjust to the time change. We dress and decide to take a long, exploratory walk. It's what we always do—walk the city, get to know it on the ground so that it begins to make sense beyond the lines on a map. We start by walking across the green expanse of Tolka Park to the Broombridge Luas station, where we purchase Leap cards for Dublin's transit system. With no car here or anywhere else on the trip, I'll be relying on buses and trains and walking. From there, we walk to Phibsborough along the Royal Canal. It's much less genteel than the Grand Canal in the south, wild and untamed, often bordered by industry rather than stately homes or picturesque pubs. Along the canal itself, though, are birdsong and wildflowers, people walking and running and biking on a beautiful Monday afternoon in June.

When we reach Phibsborough, we turn north, walking beside Glasnevin Cemetery as we loop back to where we began. Before yesterday, Glasnevin had been the outer edge of my experience with Dublin, a bus ride from city centre that at the time seemed a world away. But the fact that we had been to Glasnevin before was helpful, and I believed that having it in the general vicinity of our apartment would give me the anchor I needed. We stop for a pint at the Tolka House, for groceries at Spar, and make our way back to the apartment. My phone tells me that we've covered eight kilometres, but it feels farther. I am bone-tired and ready for sleep. As we cross Ballyboggan Road, a couple of blocks south of our flat, I notice that we have crossed into Finglas.

TUESDAY, JUNE 20, 2023

I wake in our tiny flat, unable at first to discern where I am. Sunlight filters through the slats. 5:40 a.m. I'm tired, but I know I won't get much more sleep this morning. I rise, put the kettle on for the instant coffee we bought last night, and begin to think about my day. Meet Frank Andrews at two p.m. at Strike Zone. Training tonight at Ashbourne. Without Jason Wiebe at Baseball Ireland, I wouldn't have anything on until Mariners training tomorrow night at Shanganagh Park in Shankill. Through my posts on social media, Jason became aware of what I was doing and reached out, asking if there was anything he could do to help through his position as secretary of Baseball Ireland, especially in terms of introducing me to people and setting up interviews. Then, a couple of weeks ago, we got together over Zoom so that I could give him more information about my project and he could fill me in on Baseball Ireland. As we talked, I realized that my initial interest had been centred almost completely on the club level and what baseball does for people who play at that level. As Jason talked about the national teams and about developing youth players in Ireland, I saw that I hadn't really considered these aspects or where they fit into the overall picture of baseball in Ireland or anywhere else. At one point, Jason asked why I hadn't been in touch with Baseball Ireland first. To be honest, that approach never occurred to me, so focused was I on the club level. But as we talked, it became clear that I needed to think about the relationship between the clubs and the National Team, about player development (especially at the youth level), and about how to grow the game of baseball, not only at the local but also at the national level. My conversation with Frank Andrews would be the first step in really thinking about these questions.

I leave the flat in the early afternoon and walk out to the Finglas Road, reminding myself to go to the bus stop on the left-hand side of the street. The bus tracks north, back past the Tesco, the Bottom of the Hill pub, and Mellowes Park, before it veers off on to St. Margaret's Road, past a Lidl and an Aldi and to the stop at McKelvey Avenue, in the heart of Finglas. From there, it is just a couple of short blocks' walk to Strike Zone, the Irish Baseball Institute. Once I cross St. Margaret's, I find myself on a large industrial estate. Aurora Telecom. Dunns Seafare. Warehouse after warehouse loom to my right. I turn, pass rows of transport trucks. I'm far from Elysian Fields, far from baseball's pastoral ideal, and instead deep in the grit of urban north Dublin. Finally, I see the sign for Strike Zone on the green vinyl siding of what is clearly a converted warehouse. Just down the way is the sign for the gym with which they share the space. No one is there yet, so I sit on the curb and wait for Frank to arrive.

A few minutes later, a car pulls in. A tall, wiry man wearing a light blue hoodie, black shorts, and white leggings emerges. Perched on his head is a green cap with a white harp emblazoned across it, while framing his face is a dark, bushy beard. This must be Frank. I walk up to introduce myself as a couple of teenagers unfold themselves from the back seat. Frank breaks into a smile as he extends his hand before motioning for me to follow him.

We make small talk for a few minutes before walking through the narrow corridor, past his office, and into a huge room with vaulted ceilings, twenty feet high at the side walls and rising to perhaps thirty feet at the highest point. There are a couple of throwing lanes resplendent in their green surfaces, complete with artificial mounds constructed of wood, covered in brown outdoor carpeting, and sloped down from the pitching rubber to mimic the feel of an outdoor field. There is also a place for live batting practice as well as a lane for using a hitting machine that is equipped with Hit Trax, giving players and coaches access to professional-quality feedback and statistics on exit velocity, swing path, and estimated flight of the ball. The sound of metal striking the ball's leather echoes throughout the space. Four teens are already at work, putting in reps, laughing, teasing, challenging each other to do better. I can see the display and the way it translates their physical efforts into something like a video game, a feature that I'm sure adds to the fun they are having as they put in the work on their hitting. To one side, there is also a small gym with weights and a rowing machine. The Irish tricolour with a harp superimposed on its white central area is painted on the back wall. Upstairs is a kitchen. It's a purpose-built facility, available year-round and in all weather, important considering Ireland's climate. As I will come to realize over the coming days and weeks, it's also the beating heart of development for the next generation of players in Ireland.

Frank tells me that parents don't really come around and although there are people from eight to fifty years old who at times train there, it's a space mainly run and used by teens. After he was hired in June 2020, in the midst of the pandemic, Baseball Ireland began to look for a place they could transform into what is now Strike Zone. By the fall, they had found the current location, and even though health restrictions were still in place that would severely limit its use, they pushed forward, getting the place together in about a month. When I express surprise at how fast it happened, Frank laughs and says, "But we had all the teenagers, again. So that's why. If you look around the walls, the walls are not painted cleanly, but that's teens, man. But, you know, it's energy in itself."

The teens helped create it, so it feels to them like their space, something they own and have a stake in. The laughter fades, and Frank turns serious: "It was for us, it was for them, it was for everybody. I mean, that's kind of baseball in Ireland in itself. It's not really about one person or for one person. It's everybody's group effort to just keep the sport alive and keep it going and build it."

Frank grew up playing baseball in Colorado, and his journey to Ireland and his position as Development Coach has been long and winding, taking him initially from Williston State College in North Dakota, where he played for a year, to Concordia University in Seward, Nebraska, with semi-professional summer ball back in Colorado during the summer between. While at Concordia, he contracted mono, the complications of which effectively derailed his college playing career. He did, however, graduate with a degree in Exercise Science and Biology and began to look at programs that would allow him to chart a career in sports. He landed on a Masters in Strength and Conditioning at the Limerick Institute of Technology in Tullis, County Tipperary. Sometime in that first year, one of his new friends—a Canadian—asked if he knew that there was baseball in Ireland. From there, he began to play with the Dublin Spartans while simultaneously contacting Sean Mitchell to offer his help with the National Team. He's been with them ever since, an affiliation that eventually morphed into his current role.

When Frank first started playing, it brought back memories of when he played as a kid in Colorado:

> I remember growing up, some of my favourite memories of baseball [were] just in the backyard with my friends. And that's kind of how it felt when I was over here. You know, it wasn't a lot of pressure. Everybody wanted to win, but everybody knew that it wasn't more than what it was, if that makes sense. It's everybody out on the field playing baseball. And that's the love of it, you know. They weren't there for the glory. They were there to just go and hang. Compete, but enjoy it. And that's something that I guess up until that point in my life, I had missed a lot. And that's why I want to preserve it so much.

The question for Frank, of course, then became how to keep that feeling—that focus on the fun and the positive, as well as that sense that baseball is, at its heart, still a game—but at the same time increase the calibre of play and ensure the overall longevity of the sport. How do you move beyond convincing adults to try the game, perhaps sliding over from softball, as the first generation of Irish players in the 1990s did? How do you grow the game in a country in which baseball has to compete with Gaelic football and hurling, both traditional Irish sports, as well as rugby—not to mention activities like video games—for the time and attention of children and adolescents? Where does a place like Strike Zone fit in? And why put an American expat in charge?

In listening to Frank speak, I'm struck by how much preserving that sense of baseball as he found it when he came—while still attempting to move the Irish game forward—is what animates the way he approaches his work. As we sit down in his office, away from the teenage bustle of the outer room, one of the first things he says is:

> I could have brought over a lot of American stuff and tried to make it very Americanized, but that's not the path to longevity. The path to longevity is creating it as its own culture to be respected. Even though it's strange and wonky at times, it's keeping Irish culture a part of baseball instead of removing the culture and having American baseball in Ireland.

I press him later about this difference between baseball in North America and in Ireland, but it's hard for him to put into words. Reading between the lines, it comes back to that sense of fun that dropped away after he stopped playing sandlot baseball with his friends and began to play in situations where the emphasis was on competition to the exclusion of fun. Baseball became, I think, more than just an activity, and any fun there was for him drained out. At the same time, his training—and now his job—put the increased performance of players at the forefront. When Frank says that it has to be "Irish baseball," he seems to be getting at balancing those seemingly disparate goals as a way to move baseball forward in a way that is organic to the context. As Frank later says, "I just want to see that the seeds we're putting down grow the right way."

Part of growing the game in the right way and a major force in what led to Frank's hiring and the development of Strike Zone was the creation of Baseball Ireland's 10 x 10 Strategic Plan. Developed in 2018, the goals of the plan were threefold: increase participation, improve coaching, and improve facilities. The initial goal was to increase youth participation from 150 to 1500 over a period of ten years, a strategy that was designed to sustain the game in the long term. Parallel to this focus on increased participation was an emphasis on the inclusion of a majority of home-grown players, rather than passport holders, on the National Team, in large part to provide an aspirational goal for the influx of players they hoped to see. Strike Zone is key to developing those players, but also to keeping players from straying to other sports with perhaps greater opportunities for development. In listening to Frank speak, it's clear that he realizes how important it is to create a positive atmosphere and a space to which teens will want to come. Of course, some players will fade away as other things in their lives become more important or they see baseball taking up too much of their time. But for those who are inclined to stay, Strike Zone is designed to be a space where baseball is—first and foremost—fun, and where putting in the work to get better is enjoyable.

The pandemic altered the time frame of the strategic plan, setting things back at least a couple of years, but according to Frank, it made them "re-set the right way." A lot needs to happen for participation numbers to rise, but hiring Frank and developing Strike Zone represent important strides toward two of the three goals of the 10 x 10 plan. Five players are slated to play at junior colleges in the United States in the fall of 2023, with another few likely to join them in the next few years. For a country that, before sending its first collegiate player to the US in 2022, had never developed anyone that went on to play at the university level, this was an impressive step in domestic development. When I asked Frank about these players, he was quick to emphasize that, while he had pointed out the possibility of playing college ball in the US to them, it was the players themselves who did all the legwork, dividing up the research on potential colleges and compiling it all on a shared spreadsheet, filming videos, and helping each other with the process of contacting coaches. Hearing Frank speak and later talking to these players, it's clear that Strike Zone played a large roll, not only in their dedication and development, but also in the camaraderie that developed between them and which they seem to have passed on to those a few years younger than them.

With the younger kids, Frank emphasizes playing games and having fun, alert to the fact that it's harder to keep people than it is to recruit them in the first place. To teach kids situational awareness, they use baseball5, a game played without bats or gloves in which the "batter" strikes the ball with their hand to set the play in motion. Drills are designed to be fun. Parents are not much in evidence, mostly because as people who didn't grow up with the game, they simply don't know much about it and are happy to leave Frank and the kids to it. But the upshot is that Strike Zone remains a place for the players, a place where enjoyment of the game and a sense of camaraderie sustain the hard work that is developing baseball skills.

After our talk, we walk out once more into the facility itself. There's still a group gathered around the hitting cage, taking their reps, aware of how the numbers on Hit Trax stack up against not only what they've done before, but also against their friends. A lanky young man begins to loosen in one of the throwing lanes, and a lone player does arm curls at one of the benches as the radio plays faintly in the background. More people will come once they've finished work, older players not content with training once a week, putting in reps, and getting their own feedback from Frank. I watch for a few minutes as Frank jokes with them, stopping occasionally to offer advice. As I turn to leave, Frank waves and returns to his conversation, tending the garden he's helped to plant here in the north of Dublin.

WEDNESDAY, JUNE 21, 2023

I'm sitting in Grogan's, drinking a pint of Guinness and thinking about *At Swim-Two-Birds* and its author, Flann O'Brien. Grogan's is a stop I've always made on trips to Dublin, partially because I like the way it announces itself on William Street with its deep red walls and black awnings, the white sign proclaiming it "The Castle Lounge" beckoning passing pedestrians. Its interior is anything but fancy: dark blue upholstered benches along the wall; low stools around small, round tables; a tiled ceiling that holds the remnants of the years; a long, well-lit wooden bar with its almost reverential display of bottles and its well-used taps of Guinness. This humble space was a favourite haunt of O'Brien, the pen name of Brian Ó Nualláin, or Brian O'Nolan, known also, in his writing for the *Irish Times* newspaper, as Myles na gCopaleen. As I watch the afternoon crowd, I imagine this man of many names writing in his notebook in the snug by the bar or huddled together with Brendan Behan or Patrick Kavanagh, talking about literature or just talking shite after a long day of writing. And so, visit after visit, I make my pilgrimage here, drink my pint of Guinness, and think about the Dublin that birthed so much fiction and in which so much fiction, including *At Swim-Two-Birds*, is set. Parts of the novel are actually set in Grogan's itself, a locale for drinking and conversation between the narrator—a college student and writer—and his friends.

At Swim-Two-Birds has been on my mind not only as I've thought about coming back to Dublin, but, increasingly, as I've considered this project as a whole. It's a book that contains multiple narratives, that overflows with stories that come at you as a reader in a sometimes dizzying fashion. I've been here less than two days, and the stories already seem to multiply as I meet and talk to people. At lunch, Mike Ferrato suggests that I speak with Sean Mitchell and Jaime Cuevas. A Zoom call with Jason Wiebe yields Frank Andrews, Adrian Kelly, John Dillon, and Shaun Grant, as well as a list of other names I will pursue in the next few days. The conversation with Frank circles back to stories about both Mitchell and Cuevas, while our talk also leads me to Patrick Mitchell, David Casey, Brandon Collins, Matt Dutton, and David Linn, the five young men going to play college baseball in the US. At Strike Zone, I meet players at the batting cage and parents as they drop off their kids. All of these people have stories about baseball here, in this place, just as I know there will be myriad people with stories about baseball and their experience of baseball in Scotland, Wales, and England. As these stories and possibilities of stories begin to accrete, lines from the opening paragraph of *At Swim* echo through my mind: "One beginning and one ending for a book was a thing I did not agree with. A good book may have three openings entirely dissimilar and inter-related only in the prescience of the author, or for that matter one hundred times as many endings." Here less than two days and the narrative profusion is already nearly overwhelming. I check my phone and see that I have time for another pint of plain before I need to begin the long journey south to Shankill for Mariners training.

From Grogan's, I make my way to the DART (Dublin Area Rapid Transit) station at Tara Street. The DART runs along the coast of Dublin Bay, from Malahide in the north to Greystones in the south, and provides the easiest access to the south suburbs, including Shankill where the Mariners train and play their games. The route covers familiar ground from city centre to Sydney Parade, the stop near where we stayed in Ballsbridge a few years ago. As we pass the next station at Booterstown, I can see across the sand and water of Dublin Bay to the massive towers of the Poolbeg Generating Station in the north and across to Howth in the northeast. To my right is the marsh of the Booterstown Nature Reserve. We pass Blackrock. Seapoint. Salthill & Monkstown. Teens strung out along the beach, bathing in the bay on a gorgeous summer afternoon. Dún Laoghaire, which is abustle with families and young couples walking the pier. Sandycove & Glasthule. On the coast, beyond my line of vision are the Joyce Tower Museum and the Forty Foot, detours I hope to make at some point this week. Glenageary. At Dalkey I disembark and walk down to Coliemore Harbour so that I can take in Dublin Bay for a few minutes from a stationary position. There are a lot of swimmers out today, mostly teens. The young men take turns jumping off the walls and into the water, all the while standing next to signs telling them expressly not to do so.

I return to the Dalkey station to continue my journey south. From Shankill station I walk along the bucolic Corbawn Lane to Dublin Road with its small commercial strip. Once I get to Shanganagh, I realize that the park is enormous and I have no idea where the ballfield is. Walking in, I see rugby and cricket pitches, but I'm fairly certain baseball would not be allowed in these spaces. After traversing the verge of several fields, I eventually make my way to the main parking lot. As I am trying to decide what to do, I spot a young man in a Cardinals jersey pulling a bat and kit bag out of a car. Seeing a jersey here is exceptionally rare, so I have little doubt that he will be heading to the training session. I follow him across the wide expanse of the park.

It turns out James has only been playing since seeing a notice for an indoor training program in January and has come to this particular session on his few days off between Leaving Cert exams, the final exams for Irish secondary school students. It's been, he says, a good way to meet friends, "a lot more positive than joining a football club." As we break out of the trees, I spot a rough diamond with dirt cutouts at the bases, a dirt mound, and a backstop that is about fifteen feet high, with netting around the top three fifths of its length and guy-wires anchoring it along either baseline. The outfield is just as Frank described, with flowers at the outer edges of both left and right fields and an alley of grass in dead centre field that seems to extend forever. I know that there won't be many people out tonight since the A team is playing in a European Cup Qualifier in Sweden, but a few have started to gather. A man wearing a red shirt, blue pants, and a blue Mariners hat looks up, says, "You must be Dale," and proceeds to introduce himself as Mike Mohler, coach of the Mariners' B team. Born and raised in Ireland, Mike's only been playing for five years but took over as coach of this team last year when the Mariners moved to two B teams: one that is mainly developmental for teens moving up from Cadet League, Ireland's youth circuit, and this one, which continues to be primarily comprised of rec league players.

Eight players are here tonight, including Mike and James. As people are putting on their cleats, I chat with Ed Aanstoot, a new player who has only been coming to training for a couple of weeks; while we talk, he laces up the new cleats that just came in today's mail. About a month ago he was out with his dog on the walking trails that border this field and he stopped to watch for a moment. As he stood there, one of the players said that he should come to the next training session. Intrigued, he did, telling me now that it's "great *craic*" and that "the guys have been very supportive."

There are also three American expats—James Thornton from Arizona, Shandeep "Shan" Momi from Connecticut, and a guy named Shaun from Washington—who are all in their forties and all just getting back into playing baseball after many years away from the game. James, with his salt-and-pepper beard and Mariners hat, is a fair bit older than most of the guys who I would expect to see playing ball back in Windsor. He moved from Arizona to the Netherlands to Shankill, where he, like Ed, saw the team practising in the park. In that moment, he felt the pull of baseball and decided that he wanted to take it back up because it was familiar in this place that was, in most other ways, not familiar at all. Back in Arizona, he might be playing slo-pitch softball or maybe not even thinking about baseball at all beyond watching the occasional Diamondbacks game, but here, baseball was a link to what he knew. Shaun and Shan nod as James speaks, the particulars of their stories different, but the sentiment about the familiar the same.

Before training begins, they must bring everything out from the shipping container that's tucked back in the bushes, across the walking path that runs behind the backstop and down the third baseline. The container is covered in graffiti, spray-painted tags a palimpsest that covers the original green. Inside are shovels, rakes, chalk for lines, bases, netting that can be strung across the bottom of the backstop, tarp, buckets of balls, protective screens and nets for batting practice—everything needed to maintain the field, conduct training, and play games. Together, they put up the bottom netting and put down the bases in their permanent anchors. Recent rains have made that impossible with home plate, however, so they simply throw down a temporary mat just ahead of the pool of water that occupies most of the dirt area.

Training begins with the slow, ritual jog around the outfield. Next comes group stretching, a hopeful measure of prevention against injury to aging bodies. They then pair off to play catch, arms windmilling to further loosen between tosses, distances increasing after every few throws. Mike brings them in for fielding practice, each player drifting naturally towards the outfield or infield. There's a bit of talk about who should play where, but not much, everyone settling in quickly as Mike plants himself in front of the pool at home plate and begins to hit. There's plenty of chatter about specific situations on the infield and where to throw the ball from the outfield, game simulations designed to give the players a feel—or in some cases a renewed feel—for the game. As Mike hits a sharp grounder to short, a border collie runs across the field, its owner apologetically calling the dog as play briefly ceases.

People walking along the tracks that border the field down both baselines sometimes stop to watch, curious about this sport that seems so out of place in a park in Dublin. Most, however, look up only in passing as they enjoy this beautiful summer evening and the sunshine of this longest day of the year. On the field, the players concentrate as each ball is struck, but in between there's laughter and encouragement. Shouts of "Nice play!" and "Attaway!" echo across the summer night as they strive to improve, this mixture of those just learning the game and those trying to retrieve the muscle memory of baseball from their younger selves. The three Americans have clearly played before, know to square themselves on a ground ball or hit the cut-off man at second base on a single to left field. There's definitely rust to be shaken off, but there's also an understanding of the game that comes from many days and long summer nights on the ball field. But even those who are new to the game, like young James, are making progress. He's at first base tonight, and while some balls get by him, he does make a nice play on a tricky hop. Later, he scoops the ball out of the dirt on a low throw from second base, and when he does, cheers go up around the infield. A broad smile breaks across his face. It's not an easy game to learn as an adult, but he is making strides and enjoying himself along the way.

As practice winds down and the players begin to pack up the equipment, I wave goodbye and begin the long walk back to the DART station, thinking as I go about what I've seen tonight in my first concrete experience of baseball in Ireland. Though the venue feels tentative and temporary—a pop-up field that must be created every time it is used—and the range of experience and ability of the players varies wildly, once the players took the field, nothing felt significantly different than watching at home. Baseball is baseball, no matter if the field is a purpose-built, state-of-the-art facility or a makeshift field carved out of a public park. But more than that, this was what Frank kept calling backyard baseball, the kind of baseball I remember playing with my friends when I was a kid, before everything got so serious. Tonight, fun and positive reinforcement were always at the forefront. There was no yelling, no shame in missing a play. Maybe that comes of baseball being a niche sport here, a sport that needs to be nurtured, a sport where you have to all pull together to keep it alive. Maybe all of what I saw tonight is what Frank meant when he said, "It's going to be Irish baseball." Baseball, yes, but grassroots baseball rooted in this particular place.

FRIDAY, JUNE 23, 2023

I'm standing on the Finglas Road, just outside our flat, waiting to be picked up and taken to Red Rox training in Portmarnock, a suburb on the coast nearly as far north as Malahide. A few minutes later, a car pulls up to the curb. I open the door and am greeted by John Dillon, founder of Red Rox baseball and stalwart of the national teams in the 1990s and early 2000s. He's in his early fifties, tall, slender, and square-jawed, coiled in the driver's seat as he pulls into traffic, shifts gears, introduces himself, and asks about my project. As we drive, John tells me about how he started playing the game during the early days of baseball in Ireland and how he subsequently got into coaching and working with kids, the main focus of the Red Rox organization. I begin by asking him how he started playing the game.

> I was playing softball at work with Sean Mitchell. A few of us started playing together and the next thing you know—I wasn't involved in the setting up of the National Team, but the next thing you know—we were playing for Ireland in the [1996 Qualifier for the] European Championships over in Hull in England, not knowing too much about the game. [Laughs] And that was the start

> of it, really. So that's how I got into it. I wouldn't have been a fan of baseball and that. I'm Irish-born and raised, so you know, for me it's all the other sports. I played all the other sports, you know, GAA [Gaelic Athletic Association], rugby. I played squash as well, which probably helps with the hitting. So, yeah, it was just one of those things that evolved really. I wouldn't have said I had a passion going into it or anything like that, but just found myself playing on a national team and it grew from there in terms of just enjoying it and being made to be good at it and that obviously helps with your engagement in it.

John's story is typical of the first generation of Irish-born players in Ireland who began their baseball careers in the mid-1990s and early 2000s. Softball as gateway. A history of playing other sports while growing up. Little prior knowledge of baseball. Growing into the sport even as they were thrust into the National Team.

Like many others, John went through an intense period of engagement with the sport before life intervened as he got married and started a family. He gave up baseball for a few years, but when his first-born turned five, he decided he wanted to start a kids' team as a way to give back to the game. There's a faraway look in his eyes as he begins to speak about what baseball has given him over the years:

> I'd gotten so much out of it. I'd played in the national teams for over ten years. Travelled the world, lots of European places that I just wouldn't have gone to otherwise, had some great experiences... What I found back then was amazing—

> just the eclectic mix of people in Ireland. It really represented for me the changing face of Ireland at the time, going from a very monocultural society: Catholic, predominantly white Catholic. You know, people emigrated from Ireland. Nobody came to Ireland. Just economically it wasn't viable. It was a new face of Ireland. And through baseball, you know, I got to meet—I mean, the Americans are the obvious one, but they weren't the dominant group, actually. A lot of South Americans. A lot of Europeans. Europe or baseball in Europe was kind of fast-emerging and growing at the time. Because I remember when we started, you know, the standard would have been quite poor. Over the subsequent years it elevated quite quickly.

John's desire to give back led to the formation of the Red Rox, a club with a focus on youth baseball. The club has now been in existence for ten years, but have only had an adult team in the B League for three years, a natural progression as kids got older and wanted to progress to a level beyond the Cadet League.

John finally stops the car on a dead-end street next to a low wall that borders a stand of trees. We've been driving for a half hour, north from Finglas and then east to Portmarnock. As we begin to pull equipment bags from the car, a teenager walks up the street and offers to help. John introduces him as Finn Corbett, one of the players on the Red Rox Cadet team and, as of this week, the backup catcher for the U18 National Team. Finn looks equal parts pleased and embarrassed as John lets me in on this bit of good news. I ask Finn what he likes about baseball as opposed to other sports, and he tells me that he loved it from the first day he came out at the invitation of his scout leader (now coach). From the start, he says, it was the team and the community of people that attracted him and kept him coming back. Out of the corner of my eye, I see John smile and nod.

We walk through a gap in the stone fence and into the trees, from which we emerge into a field of wild grass that reaches our waists. After a few minutes of walking, the field opens up into a rough diamond carved out of the grass, unexpected and beautiful. The backstop is comprised of three sections of netting—one directly behind home plate and two that run perpendicular from each end. Behind the backstop is a dense thicket of trees. There's a dirt mound and an area devoid of grass around home plate. Faintly painted lines extend from this area to an outfield that butts up against the tall grass. Beyond centre field is a football pitch and past that, in the distance, are the lights of the park leisure centre. I think to myself (and later post on Instagram), Is this heaven? No, it's Portmarnock.

In addition to the equipment we've dragged across the field, there is also a fenced-in enclosure where some of the larger equipment such as netting, screens for batting practice, and groundskeeping implements are stored. As at Mariners practice, the evening begins with the setup of the field, performed here primarily by the Cadet players. Someone tells me that all baseball fields in Ireland are community owned and that many of these are situated in larger public parks. That means that making improvements to them is often difficult and helps explain the provisional feel of the fields here and at Shanganagh.

The kids in attendance tonight range in age from five to sixteen, grouped by age across the three levels offered by Red Rox. Each group takes a different part of the field. Several parent volunteers supervise Coach-Pitch, for those aged five to eight, in the far reaches of centre field. John and Florian Gniech take charge of the Little Leaguers (nine- to twelve-year-olds) on the diamond proper, while Juan Lucas Galan runs the Cadets through fielding practice in right field. John throws batting practice, teaching and encouraging each batter as he or she comes to the plate, while Florian works with the fielders who try to play each at bat as if it's a game situation. It's a lot like move-up, a game I used to play with my friends at recess when we didn't have enough people for two baseball teams, with each player cycling through hitting and then into the field, moving up to each successive position in turn. It's great practice, but it's also very much a game, a fun activity that keeps the kids engaged so that they will want to return every week for training.

Two women sit in lawn chairs along the first baseline, chatting to each other while they watch John and Florian and the kids. I introduce myself, ask if they have kids out here tonight. The first to speak, Sinead Reilly, has three children in Red Rox, one at each of the levels, while the other, Breda McWalter, has a nine-year-old daughter in Little League. When I ask about their experience with baseball, Sinead replies, "The culture of this sport is different from any of the other[s] we're involved with"—less pressure and more focus on kids enjoying themselves. And with three active kids, that involvement runs the gamut of sports in Ireland. Breda tells me that her daughter loves the social aspect—the community, fun, and positivity of the coaches and club. Both emphasize how welcoming everyone is, especially the coaches, and how that contributes to a feeling of community that feels different from other sports and activities in which their kids are involved. Breda goes on to say that in baseball there's something for everybody in terms of skills, a sentiment echoed in my earlier conversations with John. It's a team game, but everyone gets their opportunity to perform individually, especially in the batter's box, and that opportunity is not dictated by level of fitness.

I sit on my hunkers as Florian yells to the shortstop, "I want you to be a crocodile." We all laugh, wondering what exactly he means, and I ask about the reactions they get when they tell people that their kids play baseball. Both mention that the response is often "There's baseball in Ireland?" and that even the staff at the park leisure centre didn't know baseball was played here when they first started coming. As Sinead notes, "It always gets conversation started."

As we watch, they occasionally ask me to explain a play on the field, tell me that even after a few years of coming out, they still don't really know the rules of the game. Neither grew up with baseball or have ever really watched it outside of these evenings and weekend afternoons with the Red Rox. And as I find out on the ride home, it's not just the parents who don't watch baseball, it's also most of the kids. They simply play the game and feel comfortable doing so having never really seen it. It's not often televised, and when it is, the time difference makes it all but impossible for kids to watch. Despite this, I'm still struck by how different this is than the experience of most kids in North America, who grow up playing *and* watching baseball, both in person and on television. Those hours of watching translate into an intuitive understanding of what's happening on the field, a cognitive mapping that for many players gets integrated with the muscle memory that's conditioned through repetition, especially in the field. Maybe that's why something like baseball5 is so crucial in teaching baseball awareness to kids who don't watch the game.

In right field Juan is working with two catchers who are taking turns receiving the ball, popping up, and throwing to second base, while at the diamond John and Florian bring the kids in to say a few words about baserunning. They end by yelling in unison, "1-2-3, Red Rox!" The kids are all smiles as they make their way to the sidelines, some searching out parents for drinks and snacks, others joking with their friends as they pack up their equipment. I say goodbye to Sinéad and Breda as their kids begin to filter over and make my way to where John is packing up the bases and balls. Having watched him work with the kids tonight, our earlier conversation in the car comes into greater focus, especially what he said about getting kids interested in baseball: "I sell it by going into a school and having the kids do it." Not by telling them why they should like it, but by showing them how much fun it can be. And that gets at the three principles that form the pillars of the Red Rox club, which together spell out the acronym RED: Respect (for teammates, coaches, and umpires), Enjoyment, and Dedication. For John and everyone else involved in the club, these three foundational ideas are integral and mutually reinforcing.

In John's eyes, the Academy (what John and others call Strike Zone) is about excellence and "Frank is about pathways for kids who can go as far as their ambitions can take them." On the other hand, he sees his own role as working to further the increased participation aspect of the 10 x 10 plan. It's about

> feeding that pipeline of players. We want to be able [...] to expand the pool of players. So that's about participation and getting as many people as possible playing baseball. So that's a key thing. Because Frank's got the excellence bit down, I can't really

> add to that. For me, where I'd like to think I could add value is, how do we get more school programs going because I know how hard it is to build a club. You can't build that overnight, so in the absence of having more clubs playing, we've talked about a ready-made structure there.

As important as the Red Rox is to John, he sees the real potential of growing the sport in getting baseball into schools through both physical education classes and school teams, or what he calls "a quicker path to building participation." The problem is that this requires a lot of volunteer hours as well as a level of buy-in from the schools that is hard to imagine at this point. As we retrace our steps across the grass field and back to the car, I look back at the field and think about what Frank called backyard baseball—what I'm coming to think of as grassroots baseball. How do you keep what's best about this iteration of the game, while at the same time growing the sport to ensure that it survives? It's a tricky balancing act that is on the minds, to greater and lesser degrees, of almost everyone I've spoken to thus far.

SATURDAY, JUNE 24, 2023

The bus ride up takes me out of Dublin, up through Finglas, and into the countryside. As we drive along the N2, we pass lush green fields dotted with sheep, horses looking off into the distance, golf and even footgolf courses. It's quiet as I alight from the bus, cross the road, and walk past the Ashbourne Community Centre.

Welcome to the International Baseball Centre. Home of Ashbourne Giants. The sign greets me as I walk through the gate and into the park. Beyond the sign lies a permanent field with a full backstop, dirt basepaths and pitcher's mound, fencing all around, wooden benches for each team along the first and third baselines, and a large manual scoreboard beyond the right field foul line. There are stands behind home plate and down the third baseline, and along the outfield fence are advertisements from local sponsors. There are houses not far beyond the outfield fences in both left and right, while beyond the fence in centre sits a copse of trees. 310 to the left field corner and 348 to the power alley in left, 317 and 331 to the corner and the alley in right, and 385 to dead centre. To the right of the field, there is a permanent batting cage and, not far from it, a pair of shipping containers for equipment. There's even a concession stand, open this morning in the lead up to today's pair of games that feature the Cork Renegades and the Ashbourne Giants in Game One, and the Mariners and the Ashbourne Titans in Game Two. It's a beautiful facility, as good as any of the amateur parks I've seen in Ontario or Michigan, and very different from the fields at Shanganagh and Portmarnock.

I wander over to the concession stand. The coffee is ready, but I'm told I'll have to wait if I want a hot dog. Just like in amateur parks everywhere. I smile to myself and wonder if they will announce over the PA, sometime in the second or third inning, that hot dogs are now ready at the concession stand.

The existence of the park at Ashbourne owes much to Sean Mitchell and his vision for the Ashbourne club and for baseball in Ireland. An original member of the Irish National Team, Sean has been involved as long as there has been baseball in Ireland. Tall and thin with short grey hair and stubble,

Sean is quick to laugh, but passionate about baseball here. As a very young child, Sean lived near Philadelphia, watching the Phillies of the '70s and playing pick-up baseball with his friends. Moving back to Ireland, there was no baseball, so he didn't pick up a bat or glove until he was asked to join a coed slo-pitch softball team at work, which soon led a number of players—including Sean, Mike Kindle, Anne Murphy, and Mick Manning, all of whom would be key members of the Baseball Ireland board—to found the first baseball league in Ireland. According to Sean, baseball in Ireland "started off with pretty humble beginnings—enough for two or three teams and, of course, no facilities, so we would just throw a few bases down in a field or just in a park."

The first purpose-built facility, Corkagh Park, was opened in 1998, funded by a donation from Peter O'Malley, owner of the Los Angeles Dodgers, through a relationship with Baseball Ireland that was forged in large part through the efforts of Anne Murphy. Perhaps as much as the facility itself, Peter O'Malley's name lent legitimacy to what they were trying to build. The creation of this facility was one of the important early steps in the development of baseball in Ireland. The development of a park like the International Baseball Centre at Ashbourne was the next logical step.

Sean played for the Dublin Spartans for twenty-two years, primarily as a catcher, and during those years also both played for and managed the National Team. In 2009, he helped form the Garristown Gruffaloes, a Little League team that moved to Ashbourne and became the Giants in 2012. By 2014, as players got older and moved through the system, the Giants were able to enter a team into the B League; by 2018, they had a team in the A League as well. Now the club fields three B teams and an A team, in addition to its youth teams in Coach Pitch, Little League, and Cadets. Like the Red Rox, the philosophy is centred on player development, with an emphasis on fun to encourage participation.

The International Baseball Centre opened in 2015, financed through a combination of fundraising and European Union matching grants: 50,000 euro was raised by the club, and 150,000 came in EU matching grants. The construction of the park has clearly allowed the Ashbourne club to flourish, but it has also facilitated the hosting of international tournaments, such as the yearly International Baseball Festival and this year's U18 European Championship Qualifier. While two purpose-built parks in all of the Republic of Ireland is clearly inadequate, the development of the International Baseball Centre at Ashbourne provides a model for the facilities prong of the 10 x 10 plan.

I grab my coffee and walk to the home bench to say hello to Jason Wiebe, who is coaching the Giants this morning. Jason looks up from the lineup card he's filling out, a wide smile across his round face, eyes alight behind his glasses, Ashbourne hat tucked low on his head. Originally from Canada, Jason has been in Ireland now for more than ten years. He talks fast, the accent as familiar as a cup of coffee from Tim Horton's, eager to talk about baseball in general and about baseball in Ireland in particular. Though he doesn't play himself, he got involved in the game while still living in Mississauga, when his son Ryan decided to play baseball rather than soccer. When he was considering taking a transfer to Dublin, he reached out to Baseball Ireland, who connected him with Sean Mitchell and the Ashbourne club. Despite not living in the immediate area, but rather in the south Dublin suburbs, Ryan began to play for Ashbourne because of its emphasis on coaching and player development. Over the years, Jason has moved from parental helper to coach of this B team and, concurrently, become increasingly involved in Baseball Ireland. Without people like him, Sean Mitchell, the woman who runs the concession stand, and so many other volunteers, baseball in Ireland would not exist.

Baseball in places like Ireland is a niche or minority sport, without the funding or infrastructure that the dominant sports—here especially GAA and, to a lesser extent, rugby—have in place. As Sean put it to me, "It's still not beyond the fragile point. It's going to be another twenty years of building strong foundations before you can trust it would be self-sustaining." The strong foundation, as far as Baseball Ireland is concerned, will develop as a result of the 10 x 10 plan, one result of which will be official recognition by Sport Ireland, along with the funding that comes along with that recognition. But that will not come until the number of participants and the number of places that baseball is played across Ireland increase dramatically. In the meantime, as Shaun Grant, president of the Dublin Hurricanes and Baseball Ireland Adult League Coordinator, told me, "As a niche sport, we're always fighting for funding, we're always fighting to keep going [...]. The sport's basically [run] on grit and passion alone."

When there's little money, the only way to get things done is through volunteer labour, and with Frank Andrews being the only employee, that means almost everything does fall on volunteers. As Shaun later said in my conversation with him, "We're all just people who love the game [...]. We all wear different jerseys, but we're all doing the same thing." Whether that is maintaining the fields or coaching or doing the league schedules, keeping score or running a concession booth or doing baseball demonstrations in schools, it's volunteers who keep things rolling along. And there are never enough of them—as Jason told me, for example, "Our biggest challenge is [getting] coaches." With only about six hundred players in the country—half of them in the youth program—there is not a huge pool of people on which they can draw. And, of course, not everyone is going to be interested in a commitment to baseball beyond playing the game, which then puts even more pressure on those who have taken on a greater burden. Whether you're talking about an individual club or baseball in the country as a whole, Sean Mitchell is adamant that "there are no short cuts here. You're looking at decades of hard slog to build a program."

I'm thinking about those links between volunteerism, baseball, and the specific contexts in which the game is played as I walk towards the open space beside the batting cage, where the Renegades are warming up. Thinking again about the idea that baseball here has to be Irish baseball. Or, as Sean Mitchell says, "Think globally about baseball, apply locally." Or, as Jason echoes, "We have to adapt to the situation we're faced with here." I'm beginning to see that particularly Irish context, but what about the differences between what each team in Dublin faces, for example? Red Rox and Ashbourne centre around youth development, while the Spartans have no youth programs at all. Drawing from central Dublin, the Hurricanes have a long history of players from South and Central America that extends to today, even though their roster is currently in transition, according to Shaun Grant. Such evolutions happen with every amateur club as people come and go and as others step from actively playing into coaching, as both John Dillon and Sean Mitchell have. Rosters change, volunteers change, even contexts and club circumstances change, but there has to be a structure in place and people willing to step up to do the work in order for it all to continue.

As I watch the Renegades play catch to warm up, I think, too, about the differences between what teams in Dublin face versus what teams in Cork in the south or Clones in County Monaghan, near the border with Northern Ireland, do. It's a shame I won't make it up to Clones, but I did have a long phone conversation with Adrian Kelly, both about their extensive Little League program and about baseball in that particular part of the country. When he talked about baseball, he made the point that it is "a sport that reaches cross community," by which he meant both religious and cultural communities, since Clones is comprised of about fifty percent foreign nationals and sits very nearly on the border. Unlike GAA or rugby in Ireland, baseball "has no baggage" in Ireland, according to Adrian. It's not a Protestant sport or a Catholic sport, a nationalist sport or a unionist sport. It can be seen as an American sport, sure, but because it's played in so many parts of the world, maybe that baggage isn't even there. It's a perspective on baseball that I would hear only from him, situated as he is in his unique geographic position. I doubt this way of thinking about baseball occurs to anyone involved in the Dublin clubs.

Cork, located as it is in the far south of the country, is also well removed from Dublin and its concerns. It's the Renegades' first year in the B League, but they are a team that's risen from the ashes of a previous team located there, the Cosmos. I've heard bits and pieces, including, from Shaun Grant, that it's "a story about how to do it right," but mostly I've been told that the Renegades should be the ones to tell their own story. I'm curious, but I'll wait until I go to Cork on Monday to talk to them about it. For today, I just want to see them play.

The Giants take the field as I settle into my seat behind home plate along with the five other people watching. The Ashbourne pitcher, Feidhlim Deering, takes his final warmup tosses, the game's lone umpire standing just to the first-base side of the mound to call balls and strikes. Cork's first batter strides to the plate but strikes out swinging on three pitches. Next to me sits a woman who is clearly the mother of one of the players, while her husband paces beside the small bleacher. I strike up a conversation, find out that their son is Miguel Ascensio, playing today in centre field, though he usually plays on the infield, at second base. He's a teenager, small, but quick. I ask how long he's been playing, and his mother tells me twelve years. He's grown up with the game, already played more baseball than many of the adult players. When they moved to Dublin, they searched to find a team where he could continue to develop and so ended up with Ashbourne. Batters two and three strike out looking. Ten pitches, three strikeouts. The fastball and slider combination have the Cork hitters fooled, at least for this first inning.

Miguel is the first batter for the Giants in the bottom half of the inning, but he hits a pop-up in the infield, as does the second batter of the inning, the third baseman, Sean O'Toole. I record their outs in my notebook, interspersing the familiar notations of scorekeeping with my ongoing notes about the game. It's a system that lets me record the plays of the game, often in a somewhat expanded form, while also noting what I see and hear around me. The result is a notational system that would probably only make sense to me.

After Feidhlim is hit by a pitch, the catcher, Jason's son Ryan, singles to the left side of the infield. Roberto Savegnago, the first baseman, works a walk to load the bases. One of the players on the Cork bench yells, "Easy out, everywhere," English momentarily breaking through the stream of Spanish chatter emanating from the Renegades' bench. But the threat dies out when Lee Edmonson pops out to his opposite number at shortstop. As the Giants take the field, so does the second umpire.

With an umpire now behind home plate, Feidhlim settles back on to the mound, ready to face the Renegades' cleanup hitter, a big, muscular man wearing #4. Solid single up the middle. When the next hitter comes to the plate, I imagine I'm seeing José Altuve bat after Aaron Judge, the contrast in size is so great. Strikeout, followed by a bunt foul with two strikes and another strikeout swinging. So far, Feidhlim's firm fastball is nicely setting up the movement of the slider.

The bottom of the inning opens with Beata Juskauskaite, the only woman playing today, hitting for the Giants. Though I will not see many other adult women playing in Ireland, female players will be common in both Scotland and England. Beata pops up to second. The next two hitters ground out to the pitcher and pop up to third base. Five pitches and the inning is over. Alec Schmidt, a right-hander, doesn't throw hard, but has been effective. The ball comes out of an overhead arm angle, but with a kind of looping motion that seems to fool the hitters, especially on the slow curve. No score through two innings.

As I watch the third inning, I'm struck by how tentative the chatter is, especially from the Giants. Even when there's a rally, there's not much encouragement, no "Come on, 1-5" or "Only you, you're the guy." No "He's afraid to pitch to you" or "Attaway, kid." Instead, it's sometimes almost silent on the field, a silence broken by players from the Cork bench cheering each other on in Spanish. It's almost like it's a part of the game that the Irish players haven't yet mastered, something they're not used to doing or don't see as part of the game. There's not even much talk on the field when a runner gets picked off first, hung up between the bases, and finally tagged out at second. Or when the first baseman makes an unassisted putout. Or when a pop-up to first base strands a runner at second.

Miguel singles to start the Giants' half of the third. His mom claps and cheers, while his father just smiles as he leans over the back of the bleacher. He moves to second on a balk call, the umpire stopping to re-explain the rule to the pitcher. A strikeout and hit batter put runners on first and second before Ryan hits a solid single to left to score the first run of the game. Maybe they've figured out the Cork pitcher. And sure enough, Roberto hits a hard liner to the left side, but the third baseman, Filip Zakrocki, moves quickly to his right, leaping to snare the ball before calmly pivoting to throw the ball to second base to complete the double play. It's a great piece of fielding, and the Cork players let him know, pounding him on the back and high-fiving him as they run off the field.

After a strikeout to start the inning, Zakrocki beats out an infield single, steals second, and then takes third on a ball in the dirt. The next batter walks and steals second, putting runners at second and third. Cork is threatening to take the lead. One of the Ashbourne bench players who has drifted over to the bleachers to talk with his friends says, "I want to get intentionally walked, but I won't. I'm only a threat to myself." A run scores on a ball in the dirt, with the other runner moving up to third. K for out number two, but then an error by the shortstop allows the go-ahead run to score. From second base, Beata calls to her teammates about what they should do depending on where the ball is hit. Someone on the Cork bench yells to the batter, the only clearly novice hitter in the Renegades' lineup, "Nothing above the shoulders. It's not hurling." Despite the advice, he strikes out, ending the threat. Cork leads 2–1.

Schmidt continues to drop his curve in for strikes. It's a pitch that often fools the Giants' hitters, messing with their timing so that when they make contact, they only get part of the ball, resulting in either groundouts or lazy pop flies. This inning, it's the groundouts, resulting in two outs with a runner on first. That brings up Jack O'Reilly, the number nine hitter, who just recently moved up to the B League from Cadets. He nubs the ball, a squib past the pitcher, but too soft to be playable by the second baseman. It's an infield single, Jack's first ever hit in the adult league. The next batter hits another ground ball to third for the final out. As Jack turns back from second and trots in to retrieve his glove, Jason holds up a ball, indicates it's from the infield single. A huge grin spreads across Jack's face as he stares at the ball in Jason's hand, this memento of his move from youth to adult baseball.

Adrian Kelly first tried baseball at a stag night at a facility in Galway called Pure Skill, which offers ten different sporting challenges, including a batting cage. A couple of weeks after hitting all ten balls that first night, Adrian saw a baseball team marching in a St. Patrick's Day parade and, interest piqued, decided to go along for training. Shaun Grant—now busy with the Dublin Hurricanes and at Strike Zone—was first exposed to baseball on a trip to Florida and thought to himself, I can do this. Once he decided to play, he searched out and joined the Hurricanes, drawn in by the idea that you don't have to be a perfect athlete to play the game. As he said to me when we spoke at Strike Zone, "That's the joy of baseball, that it doesn't really matter how you are, how you grew up, or your physical ability. There's always something you can do." Sean Mitchell and John Dillon came over from softball. Others came to baseball through friends or just happened to see a team practising in their local park or had played in another country and wanted to get back into the game. Miguel Ascensio's parents sought out baseball when they moved to Ireland, as did Jason Wiebe for his son Ryan. But chance encounters with baseball, people moving from other sports, and immigrants who already played baseball before moving to Ireland are not enough to increase participation or even to keep the sport at its current level. Getting Irish-born kids like Jack into baseball is what is needed to sustain and grow baseball in the country.

While the Mariners and Hurricanes have Little League teams, both began as adult teams, with the youth programs developing later. The Ashbourne and Red Rox clubs, on the other hand, began with youth programs and then added adult teams as the kids progressed through the system. As Sean Mitchell said, "Start with kids and as they grow up—you know a lot of the A team are those kids who started in 2009 [...]. You get the kids coming up, you mix in a few experienced players in with them." In both models, if it's working correctly, the youth and adult programs will benefit from each other in a cross-pollination that makes each better. As well, it's these kids who have come up through these youth programs who train at Strike Zone and who have begun to filter into the National Team. But however they come about, youth programs at the club level require a massive amount of volunteer involvement, not only from coaches, but also the people needed to do demonstrations of baseball in the schools in order to get the word out about baseball and recruit new players in a country where baseball has almost no visibility. In Shaun Grant's words, before he started playing, he "didn't really know that baseball was a thing here." Most people don't.

But as necessary as the youth programs are to developing and sustaining both individual clubs and, eventually, the National Team, everyone at Baseball Ireland came to the realization that club baseball itself would not be enough to reach the goals laid out in the 10 x 10 plan. Again, here's Sean Mitchell: "On the membership growth side of things, we concluded that that kind of pace of growth of 10X in ten years is not going to be possible organically through the clubs. There's only so much that the clubs could even absorb." And additional clubs would need "a driving force on the ground," the kind of volunteer commitment that cannot be compelled. Instead, schools were seen as the route to establishing this rapid pace of growth. The dream is to get into physical education classes and, beyond that, to get school teams set up so that kids have a competitive alternative to the club system, which would be run in parallel. The first step, though, is going into schools and showing the kids (and their teachers) that baseball is a thing here. As John Dillon told me, kids get a lot out of it, especially when they get to try hitting. Adrian Kelly told me much the same thing, emphasizing that going into schools and getting the kids involved is a way to establish credibility with not only the kids, but with parents and teachers as well. Parents and teachers see the benefits of baseball in that not every kid is suited to GAA or football or rugby, both in terms of fitness, but also in terms of skill sets. It's a team sport, yes, but the place of the individual—in the batter's box several times per game—is also at the heart of the game. In John Dillon's words, "Everyone does still get the opportunity to have an at-bat [...]. It's the equivalent of kicking a penalty, right, but everyone does not get the opportunity to kick a penalty."

What all of these people are saying, I think, is that if kids can be exposed to baseball in meaningful ways, then they might see a place for themselves in the game. Like Jack with his first hit or Feidhlim with his slider.

It's 2–1 Cork in the top of the fifth. A close, low-scoring game—not what I'd been led to expect from seeing league scores before making the trip or in talking to people like Shaun Grant, who told me that "this is a league of hitting [...]. If you're not scoring ten, you're not winning a lot of games." But a close game can turn quickly. The Cork half of the inning starts with a single and a walk, followed by another strikeout, their sixth of the game. Overhead, planes climb out of Dublin airport, contrails stark against the blue. The Renegades' coach yells, "One out. Let's do this," encouraging his team in a mix of Spanish and English. With the fourth batter of the inning at the plate, the lead runner appears to be picked off second, but the shortstop freezes and never throws the ball to third base. Instead, it's a steal and runners are now at second and third. The batter walks, but the catcher makes a snap throw to third that the third baseman can't handle. 3–1 Cork. From there the floodgates open, a combination of walks and errors in the field. The Renegades capitalize on every mistake, and by the time the inning ends, the score is 9–1 Cork.

The Mariners and Titans have started to filter in for the next game. David Linn, one of the young guys going over to college in the US, stops to say hello. I've seen him around Strike Zone a couple of times, always laughing with his friends, always upbeat, and *always* ready to talk. He's been playing baseball since he was six and moved to Ireland when he was twelve, playing with Ashbourne from the start. Though there's an American accent underneath, you can hear the six years of being in Ireland in his voice, especially when talking about the recruitment video he made: "I sent it to a good few colleges." It's not only the phrasing, but also the slight lilt when he says words like *colleges*.

Over the course of our many conversations, David talks mainly about Strike Zone, about his peers and the younger kids coming up behind them, and about his relationship with baseball. He's happiest when he's at the facility, trying to get better so that he can "play baseball at the highest level," the first step of which for him is junior college in Illinois. It's not only the facilities available at Strike Zone, but also the coaching that Frank is able to offer that has made the difference for him and the rest of the teens who haunt the place every day. You can see that in the decision Patrick Mitchell, the first Irish player to play college ball in the US (and Sean Mitchell's son), made to forego an offer to play summer collegiate baseball so that he could instead come back to Dublin to work with Frank and train with the guys he came up with.

In training together, the older teens have been able to both push and support each other. But it's the players behind them—those who are fourteen, fifteen, sixteen—to whom David Linn keeps returning, anticipating everything that David Casey, the only one of the players headed to junior college in the US who has never lived outside of Ireland, will tell me the next day. The two Davids, as I come to think of them, are, in many ways, very different from one another—Casey, tall and thin, with a mop of curly brown hair, is soft spoken and laconic, and needs to be drawn into conversation, while Linn, more compact, with a nervous energy coiled inside him, is always talking, always instigating conversation. The pitcher and the shortstop. But both are passionate about baseball, not only in their own lives, but also with regard to baseball in Ireland.

Of those younger players, David Casey tells me, "They're not messing around, but they're still having fun while they're doing it. They're loving the game, but more importantly they're loving the process. They love putting in the work because they can see it and they've experienced the benefit first-hand. They trusted the process." David Linn: "They're trying to get better—they know what they're doing [...]. They'll come in and they'll just dominate the adults because they've been able to have that training." I'm struck by the concern and regard the two Davids have for those coming up behind them. And it's not just these two; when I chat with Feidhlim and Ryan later that day, it's not the game they played today they want to discuss—perhaps understandable given the score—but instead they want to talk about Strike Zone, how important it has been as a space for the young guys to train together, and how they have all learned and progressed through their time there. Not only are they all focused on their own baseball careers, but as the first generation of players to train at Strike Zone, they seem to understand and accept the responsibility they have to the larger project of baseball in Ireland. For all of them, that means supporting the kids who are coming behind them, an expression of Shaun Grant's sentiment that "our sport is a great community."

I ask David Linn: "What is it about baseball? Why is baseball so important to you?" He's silent for a minute, the first time I've seen him at a loss for words. Then he begins to speak:

> I love baseball. It's like—I don't know. It's unmatched. I can't even really put it into words. It's just—I don't know. Honestly, I don't know why. It's just what I love. I couldn't tell you or put it into words. It's just baseball, you know what I mean?

> Like, baseball, whether it's over here or in the States or whether it's wherever. It's just amazing. It's all I've ever wanted to do, it's all I ever think about.

Or, as baseball writer Sarah Langs so often says, "Baseball is the best."

As we talk, the Giants score a run to make it 9–2, but the rally ends with a runner doubled off second after the second baseman catches a line shot. David turns to me and says, "If you make the routine plays, you'll do well here."

The game progresses with Cork able to make those plays while the Giants cannot. The game ends 18–2 after six innings when the mercy rule is applied.

As I'm sitting on the bleachers taking notes between games, one of the Giants comes over, introducing himself as Jack O'Reilly. Cap askew, uniform dirty from the game, he's still buzzing from collecting his first hit, all smiles as he sinks into the bench beside me. He asks why I'm taking notes, what I'm writing about. I tell him about how I'm writing a book about baseball in Ireland and Scotland and England and Wales, and that I'm interested not only in what baseball looks like here, but in why people play it. Jack tells me that he is autistic and that baseball is a good game for autistic people because there is no physical contact. Autistic people, he tells me, don't like physical contact. But baseball is also a good game because there's more than one way to be good at it. Talking to Jack brings me back to my conversation with John Dillon, who also spoke about the lack of physical contact in baseball and about the ways in which it's a good game for kids on the autism spectrum because "it gives them an opportunity to play a team sport, but focus individually." What both John and Jack are talking about is the way that baseball is, or can be, inclusive, a sport in which the idea of participation is not just bound up in numbers, but also in *who* is able to play the game. Before Jack ambles off in search of some post-game food, he tells me that there are three people on his team who have autism and that one day he would like to play on a team comprised exclusively of people with autism.

We're back to one umpire for the next game, balls and strikes again being called from the field. Mike Mohler leads off for the Mariners in the top of the first, drawing a walk before stealing second, advancing to third on a passed ball, and scoring on a wild pitch. David Linn is catching, a position with which he's not at all familiar. But without Cian Fowler, a fifteen-year-old who is their regular catcher, in attendance, I can imagine David in Sean Mitchell's ear, cajoling him into letting him catch. Already, though, I can see it's going to be a long afternoon for him. A combination of walks, errors, and timely hits add up to a 4–0 lead by the time the Titans come to bat.

The Titans load the bases in the first, with David reaching on an error, Noah Pinto on a single, and Damian Pruszowski on a walk. With two outs, Sean Mitchell comes to bat. You can tell Sean has played a lot of baseball from the way he sets himself in the field and his approach at the plate. He's patient, waiting for a pitch he can hit. And hit he does, a long fly ball that the right fielder is able to track down. Three runners stranded. Still 4–0 Mariners.

When I speak with David Casey, I ask him about the guys a year or two younger than him and whether he thinks there's going to be another crop of players willing and able to go to the US to play college ball. He's animated as he answers the question, his words coming more quickly than they have at any other point in our conversation.

> Oh yeah, God, names like Cian Fowler. Noah Pinto. Cian Fowler is doing his Junior Cert, and he's catching people like Patrick [Mitchell] and myself and Liam who are guys throwing in the 80s [...]. He's the youngest player or the second youngest on the A team. He's got one of the highest batting averages [...]; he's only struck out maybe two or three times. That's insane, right? I love having him as my catcher because, first of all, he's very smart. Fourteen, fifteen, and he's calling great games. He just knows what to do.

A few weeks later, at the British Baseball Federation Summer Cup in Slough, I'm able to catch up with Cian's father, David. He tells me that Cian started playing when he was seven, the result of a leaflet being dropped at school. He and his wife at first said no, since Cian was already involved in both GAA and football, as well as swimming and piano. But Cian insisted, attending summer camp and then becoming obsessed with the game. David tells me Cian "dropped GAA like a hot potato. He plays football only because it doesn't interfere with his baseball training. I've never seen anyone as passionate about something." It's a stark contrast to most of the kids who play here; because the game is not really available to watch, it's sometimes a case of out of sight, out of mind. As Sean Mitchell puts it, "They don't have those kinds of role models. They have to learn the game from the ground up here." Those who do become serious, though, surrounding themselves with the game and with others who are equally into it, like the other teens who train at Strike Zone.

It's the support and cohesion of these teenage players that comes across most forcefully in talking with David Fowler. You can see the wonder in his eyes when he starts to speak about them. "The kids that play—the temperament of the kids, the camaraderie of the kids that play—I helped out in every sport [Cian] did, and there's nothing like you see in baseball." He mentions people like David Linn, David Casey, and Patrick Mitchell, adding that "in football, you never get the older lads hanging back to try and help the younger lads." I think back to what Sinead Reilly told me at Red Rox training about the culture of baseball in Ireland being different than those of the other sports in which her kids are involved.

What has developed organically at Strike Zone through Frank's coaching and presence, the atmosphere that has naturally evolved, and the dedication of the young players is a baseball culture that must already exceed what Baseball Ireland envisioned when they set it up. In the three prongs of participation, coaching, and facility development, Iceland soccer was seen as the model, but in terms of baseball culture and the development of a national team, they looked to Austria. The Austrian team are all domestic guys who train together as a team. No passport holders, no mercenary approach to climbing the European and World rankings, but rather developing homegrown players for the National Team and ensuring that a high percentage of the team will be drawn from those domestic players, a percentage set to increase each year. It's part of the plan to grow the game and sustain that growth by giving the best domestic players a pathway to the National Team. As Sean Mitchell says, "If there's blockage there where they can't even get a chance on the National Team, it's highly damaging." As Todd Westover, another parent, put it when I spoke to him the following weekend, "Some of the kids here are playing ten, eleven months a year. Training. How are you going to take that away from them? And what is that going to do to baseball by not letting them compete for their country?" By severely limiting the number of Irish passport holders who reside in other countries on the Irish National Baseball Team, the aim is to open up that path for the best home-grown players, those who have come up through the developing youth programs and Strike Zone.

Baseball Ireland were worried at first that they wouldn't be able to develop national calibre pitching and would continue to have to rely on passport holders, but the young players coming up have shown that such worries are unfounded. "What's changed," according to Sean, "is we now develop athletes." Facilities and coaching lead to this kind of development. You can predict that. But what you can't predict, I don't think, is the culture that has been created along with that player development. To my mind, this culture of support and camaraderie is at least as important and will continue to pay dividends in the coming years.

The game ends 18–15 Mariners. As in the first game, the mix of skill levels within each team is quite evident. It is, indeed, "a league of hitting," one in which the team best able to perform the fundamentals is the team most likely to win. Throw strikes. Hit the ball. Make the plays you're supposed to make. That's what wins games, here or wherever. Baseball is baseball.

CORK

Everybody's different, but we all come
together for a love of baseball.

—BRETT SUTHERLAND, PRESIDENT,
CORK RENEGADES

THURSDAY, JUNE 29, 2023

A dark-coloured Nissan Cube stops next to me as I stand beside the north branch of the River Lee, at the edge of Cork's city centre. Traffic in this part of town is intense, a jumble of one-way streets and impatient drivers. I know it's the right vehicle when the window rolls down and I'm told to hop in. It's my ride to Renegades training at Tramore Valley Park on the far south side of the city.

As I get in the car, I'm hit with a sonic wave, the wall of guitars from Sleep's *The Sciences* blasting from the car's speakers. The passenger turns around, talks over the music to introduce himself as Filip Zakrocki and the driver as Matt Altman. I recognize both of them from the first game at Ashbourne on Saturday—Filip had a couple of hits and in the field had the look of someone who was not new to the game, while Matt was memorable for having been hit twice in his two at-bats. The second time it happened, he pantomimed being struck down by a much faster pitch, then walked out and hugged the Giants' pitcher. Matt wears shorts over black-and-gold striped leggings, a Renegades hat and sunglasses, and a sleeveless hoodie over which a cross is draped. A tattoo of a snake curls around his left forearm. Strands of long blond hair escape from his cap above a face framed by an impressive goatee. As he drives, he takes frequent pulls from a disposable vape, an accessory that seldom leaves his hand.

While Matt manoeuvres out of the city centre traffic, Filip turns in his seat to ask more about what I'm doing here in Cork. He's wearing a black hoodie that says, *RENEGADES BASEBALL EST. CORK 2022*, a Renegades hat, and black shorts. He is square-jawed and clean shaven, with a smile that I will rarely see leave his face—like Matt's ever-present vape—over the next several days here and back in Dublin. He seems genuinely curious about my interest in baseball over here in general and in Cork in particular, and as what I'm doing becomes clearer, both he and Matt begin to offer their stories. Both are from Poland originally but have been living in Cork for more than eight years. Filip has been playing baseball for twenty years, since he was thirteen, and played in the Ekstraliga, the highest level of baseball in Poland, before moving to Ireland. Matt, on the other hand, only took up the sport a couple of years ago when Filip encouraged him to come out to training. That was with the Cork club that folded before the formation of the Renegades. Bits and pieces of that story emerge as we talk, but our conversation is cut short as we pull into the parking lot at Tramore Valley. I still only have a vague outline of what happened and the origins of the Renegades.

A few days ago, we took the train from Dublin to Cork, a scenic three-hour ride through lush, green fields—exactly what the mind conjures when most people think of Ireland. But as I looked out the window at that landscape, I kept thinking that Cork to Dublin was a long way for the Renegades to travel, especially when the journey would not be the bucolic experience I was having, but instead would feature motorways, laybys, and city traffic. Distance from Dublin alone means that it takes a high degree of commitment to play baseball in Cork. As in most things, bridging the distance between Cork and Dublin is not in any way easy.

I've spent the days since we arrived walking the city, absorbing it as much as I can in the days before I would meet the Renegades. We walked from where our hotel sits just west of Fitzgerald Park east to city centre with its tightly woven streets between the two branches of the River Lee. I sat and watched the array of people and the enormous ravens that frequent the Grand Parade, walked the length of Oliver Plunkett Street, with its shops and restaurants and buskers and summer crowds. We ambled south and east to University College Cork, an idealized picture of a university. We wandered through the residential neighbourhoods of Cork Lough, watching the birds as we traversed the path around the lough. We took the bus to Blackrock, on the east side of the city, and walked along the river with its mixture of parkland and industrial spaces. Cork has a much different feel than Dublin—grittier, more eclectic in its architecture, the mix of building styles endlessly fascinating to me. Though they are often seen as residents of the second city of Ireland, Corkonians do not at all see themselves that way. It's not an easy position to occupy—like that of Chicago in relation to New York—but it's especially pointed in Ireland, where the animosity is longstanding and still runs deep. As I walk, I think about the divide between the two cities, as well as the distance between them, and wonder what effect it has on trying to establish baseball in Cork when the hub of baseball activity is and, to a large degree, always has been Dublin.

Tramore Valley Park is another enormous park without any designated space for baseball, but it's here that the Renegades train once a week, though they play their games at Brian Dillon GAA field, a pitch they currently rent on the city's north side. Here they also set up their equipment—all of which has been carted to the grounds by members of the team—on what also appears to be a GAA pitch. To one side, three people stand in a triangle, knocking a *sliotar*—the ball used in hurling—between them with their hurleys. On the other side, on an embankment just above the Renegades' training space, there's cross-country training. It is very much a multi-use park, functional but not at all ideal for their needs.

There are twenty-two people here tonight, some of whom train with the team but do not play in games, a consequence of currently having only one team in the B League in this, their first season playing competitive games. They already have forty people on the active roster and another fifteen to twenty who sometimes come to training on Thursdays, with tonight's total slightly higher. There is also training on Monday nights, but that time is reserved for the more experienced players. Brett Sutherland tells me that Filip, who was a very successful pitcher in Poland, "can throw a ball so fucking hard" that it's not safe for novices. Among their members, the Renegades count people from twenty-two countries, an eclectic mix of people who, I'm told, "all come together for a love of baseball." At this point, they are an adult team, comprised of people from different homelands looking for an outlet to play baseball.

The training session begins with the team in a circle for announcements. Brett calls for quiet and begins: *First, I'd like to welcome the new people who are out tonight. As well, I'd like to introduce and welcome Dale Jacobs, who is writing about baseball in Ireland. He'll be observing tonight and may want to speak with some of you. Okay, game this weekend in Dublin against the Mariners. How many cars? Who's driving? It's an eleven a.m. start, so we'll need to leave by seven a.m. at the latest. Plan to be back late. And don't forget the barbeque after the next home game on July 23. Be sure to bring your families. Okay, let's start with stretching.* As they settle in to stretches and then pair off for warmup tosses that get progressively longer, I walk around the edges of the field, watching the arc of the balls as they fly back and forth. I hear Arturo Ocaña explaining to tonight's new players why one finger should be placed outside the glove. I spot the players for whom baseball is all muscle memory and the ones who are just learning to throw and to catch. Experience with the game varies wildly, just as it has in all the clubs I've seen thus far.

Brett Sutherland is a bundle of energy, pinballing between groups of players, taking part in various drills, all the while juggling multiple conversations across the training ground. Despite being in his early forties, he's out at the front when the teams does sprints to start the practice. One minute he's laughing like a kid, taking obvious joy in being out on the field, and the next minute, he and Marco Sibillano are discussing how to teach some of the new players to grip the ball correctly when throwing. I see what he means when he says he regards the Renegades as "serious fun."

When I'm finally able to corral Brett for a few minutes, I ask about his background in baseball and about the formation of the Renegades. Though he played cricket when he was younger, it wasn't until he was thirty-one, while living in France, that he discovered baseball. From the moment he picked up a glove, he was in love with baseball and with learning a new sport. Over the next ten years, as he moved around for his job, he would train with teams in the UK and Ireland—wherever he happened to be—before finally settling in Cork and becoming a member of the Cork Cosmos, the predecessor to the Renegades. There were, however, a lot of problems with the Cosmos, both with the relationship its manager had with the team and with the league as a whole. Brett describes the former manager as a dictator who would brook no questions about how he was running the team: "It was a regime, and he was so oppressive [...]; nobody would be smiling. If you were laughing, he'd be 'What the fuck are you laughing for?'" As we speak, I can hear laughter and happy banter as the players work through fielding drills.

The league finally had enough of his behaviour and kicked him out; at that time, a committee was formed to try to manage the team. Brett and others were part of that committee, but were, in Brett's words, "just puppets." The Cosmos were allowed back in the league, but finally banned the former manager for multiple cases of lying. It was then that Brett, Andrés Fornes, and Tommy Billi came together to form a new team, the Cork Renegades. Speaking with Adrian Kelly about the formation of the Renegades on the Baseball Ireland Podcast, Brett said, "Here's an opportunity to right the wrongs of the previous team and perhaps try to offer people in Cork who want to play baseball something legitimate, something credible, something comprehensive, and where they can have their own voice. Because a lot of our voices got lost in the previous team—drowned out."

Andrés was tapped to be the head coach, with Marco as his assistant. When I meet Andrés and he sees that I am wearing a Detroit Tigers cap, one of the first things he tells me was that he is originally from Maracay, Venezuela,

Miguel Cabrera's hometown. After a few minutes, discussion of Miggy and in between shouts of encouragement to players taking infield, he fills me in on his background in baseball. He started playing at six, and at fifteen he attended one of the Venezuelan baseball academies, hoping to catch on to the minor leagues. After unsuccessful tryouts with a half dozen major league organizations, he moved to playing baseball at Simón Bolívar University in Caracas. After he graduated, he moved to Argentina, but did not play baseball there. It was when he was living in Portugal that he began training with the Loulé Ravens, getting back into baseball after an absence of a couple years.

When he moved to Ireland a year and a half ago, however, Andrés thought that he would be hanging up his cleats for good. But then a friend named Alejandro Rodríguez mentioned that he played for a team called the Cosmos. Then, when things began to happen with the formation of the new team, everything started moving very quickly. He was asked to speak with Eric Kelly about coaching, but when Eric bowed out because of family and business commitments, Andrés realized that, since there was no one else, it had to be him, even though he had never coached before at any level. When I ask about the transition to coaching, he tells me,

> It was really hard at the beginning, because when you are a player, you only focus on your performance, but here you have to be attentive to the pitcher—how is the pitcher performing, knowing when to step in and change him for another one—giving all the time instructions to the players of what to do, where to locate, and, you know, doing a lot of things that are in the field and out

> of the field at the same time. And sometimes you forget about what you, in your position, are going to do in the next play.

In addition to Marco as his assistant coach, he has people like Alejandro, who often acts as his bench coach, giving him advice on personnel in game situations. The Renegades have been an unexpected opportunity to stay connected to the game he loves. "Baseball," he tells me, "has been the best thing in my life." He goes on to say, "What made me fall in love with baseball itself was when I started this entire project of the Renegades. I was able to see baseball from another point of view."

Meanwhile, Brett was asked to spearhead the project as the general manager and face of the team. With his first child on the way, Brett was hesitant, but finally agreed. Before he goes on, we stop for a minute to watch Andrés take batting practice. He's got some pop, spraying the ball to all fields as he takes his reps. Brett looks back from the field, tells me, "If I don't do it, no one's gonna do it. Friends, including myself, wouldn't have anywhere to play. We just wouldn't. There'd be nothing and it would die. And I love the sport. I live for this game." He points at the coach, tells me that he and Andrés are here to stay—"Ireland is my forever home"—and that they want to build this team so that there is a sustained presence of baseball in Cork. He, Andrés, and Roemer Pompa, the club's treasurer, "talk all day, every day about what's next," but, especially because of the way the previous team was run, they want to make sure that the voices of all the players are heard.

Matt is just finishing his turn at bat. Brett tells me that he's switched from batting left to batting right this year and has had to completely re-learn his swing. No explanation is offered for this radical change, and I wonder if Brett even has one. As Matt stands at the plate, I remember him as the player who got hit twice on Saturday. On the ride home later, I ask him about how he feels and if he's been hit before. There's a mischievous look as he laughs and tells me that he gets hit all the time. He confirms that his ribs are still sore, but he also seems a bit proud of his penchant for wearing pitches.

Brett and I end our conversation so that he can take his turn at batting practice now that Matt has finished. He's one of the few who doesn't wear gloves. Old school. I watch as he makes solid contact on the first couple of pitches, then I begin to wander around the rest of the training. Arturo Ocaña stands next to me as I watch, telling me that he spent six months in Detroit working on a contract in IT. It's good to talk with someone who is familiar with Detroit, which sits just across the river from my home in Windsor, Ontario.

I also speak with Heidi Bodin, who is originally from Denmark. Unlike most of the expats here, she didn't grow up with baseball, though she did play rounders on Sundays as a child. She was intrigued by baseball, seeing it as a way to both get some exercise and to meet new people. The social aspect is so important to her that she has taken on the coordination of the team's social events that happen outside the baseball diamond. Andrés stresses to me the importance of the social aspect of the club to the majority of the players:

> I think we're like a family, and I know you probably get this answer a lot. For most of the people within the team, baseball and the Renegades is pretty much all they have, socially speaking. I think that was a really eye-opening thing for us.

> We're always very active in that way, and [we try] to enjoy as much as we can the experience in general, not just within the field. And I think that has helped us a lot within the field because we have a better chemistry.

Or as Kai Gao, the Renegades' middle infielder turned pitcher, tells me later, "We're not just playing baseball. It's also a good opportunity for me to know all those people from everywhere. To have friends. To communicate with people—the third important thing as a human being, after food and water." Clearly, the Renegades are a bigger part of people's lives than something to do a couple of days a week.

Towards the parking lot, Filip is just finishing his bullpen. I see the easy velocity of his throws, hear the crack when it lands in the catcher's mitt. Without a doubt, he throws much harder than most of the B league pitchers I've seen thus far. Kai Gao walks over to say hello. He's a smooth middle infielder, but has also started to work out as one of the Renegades' pitchers. I'm surprised when he tells me that he's only been playing baseball since he moved to Ireland a few years ago and only began playing softball as a freshman at Xiamen University in his native China. In his three years on the university team, he benefitted from having experienced coaches from Taiwan. Of that experience playing softball, Kai says, "In the first two years, I was so passionate about [softball], so I always [thought] about it even when I was in class." Softball, and later baseball, captivated him from the beginning, whether playing in games or just throwing the ball around between a couple of people.

Initially playing with the Mariners in Dublin, he joined the Renegades when he moved to Cork for work this spring. "The day I arrived in Cork—I remember it was May 25—

and that's also the day they have training. So I arrived in Cork around three [...]. I rented a new place and ran to put all my stuff there and just ran to the training with the Renegades." Everything else could wait, but baseball could not. Curious, I press him to tell me what it is about baseball, and he replies, "Every week, I always look forward to the training. [Baseball] just purely makes me much happier. Sometimes I eat vitamins—if I play baseball, I don't really need it." He laughs as he says these final words, his joy at the game palpable. Like David Linn, he can't quite put it into words, but he knows how important baseball is to him and that it's one of the things that makes him truly happy. When I ask him about this team, he replies, "We play with respect for everyone, and we encourage everyone. The best quality of this team is that when we make mistakes, [the other players] don't blame you. Always encouraging you. 'Forget it. Forget it. It was just a mistake.' I would say that's the best thing about this team." In addition to the social aspect of the Renegades, the team provides a supportive atmosphere in which he can pursue the game he loves.

As Filip throws his last pitch, Kai breaks off the conversation so that he can start his own bullpen session. They are all throwing off flat grass since there is no mound at Tramore Valley Park, though they have put down a pitching rubber and measured off sixty feet, six inches. A right-hander, Kai begins in an upright position, part of his right foot touching the rubber, right leg slightly bent. His hand is in his glove at the letters. His motion is a slow step forward as he pushes off with his right foot. He doesn't have Filip's speed, but he's hitting the glove, and at this level, that's the main prerequisite for a pitcher.

As Kai throws, I chat with Alec Schmidt while he waits to throw; he, Kai, Filip, and Andrés form the team's pitching staff. His twin brother Ryan is the team's primary catcher and is behind the dish right now. They're both from Ireland and have lived here all of their lives, but they learned baseball through extended family summers in New Jersey, exposure to the game that is unusual for Irish kids. Neither could get the game out of their system, and they both jumped at the chance to play when the Renegades were formed. Their father is one of four sponsors who help the team out with apparel and equipment costs, as well as providing concessions for players who are unable to afford either the league fees or the weekly training cost of four euro. Maybe it's only because the team is so new, but there's a palpable excitement as I talk to the players, and as Brett said to me, they do indeed seem to have each other's backs.

Like Sean Mitchell, Brett realizes that baseball is "not entrenched in Irish culture" and that its continued existence is by no means guaranteed. The philosophy with the Renegades is that coaching needs to happen in a fun, accessible way that yields individual improvement, but does so in a way that's also enjoyable for players, ensuring that they will continue to come out to training every week. Having seen them play in Ashbourne and now watching this session, it's obvious that they want to win and that they want to improve, but it's also clear that the players are here to have a good time and to enjoy each other's company. Many of these expats are quite experienced, having played baseball as kids or young adults before coming to Ireland. Although they plan to start a youth program, the team right now is strictly for adults. Higher on the priority list, though, are a team in the A league and, perhaps, a second B team so that they can accommodate all of the adults who come to training but are not yet able to play in games.

The highest priority, however, the one that Brett and Andrés and Roemer think about and discuss most often, is where they will be training and playing their games in the future. Their current situation—training here at Tramore Valley and games at Brian Dillon GAA Field—is the result of actions taken (or, in this case, not taken) by the previous management. The Cosmos had use of a suitable field for both games and training in Carrigrohane, a village just west of Cork City, but when the Renegades were setting up, they discovered that the rent on the facility was in serious arrears and that even with repayment of what was owed, they were no longer welcome. They've been meeting with local counsellors, trying to get them to see the value in baseball so that they will be on board, but nothing is yet certain. The issue of where to play and the lack of dedicated facilities is one I've heard multiple times since I arrived and one that I will continue to hear over the course of the summer in every locale and with every team I visit.

As I ride the train back to Dublin for another weekend of games, I think once again about the distance from Dublin to Cork. It's not only geographic distance, an enormous impediment in and of itself, but also a distance of approaches. The Renegades are coming at baseball in their own way, a way that suits the community in which they are located—and, with Brett Sutherland and Andrés Fornes, are doing so with not one, but two of what Sean Mitchell called "driving forces on the ground." Despite many similarities to clubs elsewhere in Ireland, the leaders of the Cork team look to Dublin with a bit of a chip on their shoulders, perceiving what's happening there as indicative of a larger club to which they are struggling to be admitted. There is, I think, a reason that they decided to call themselves the Renegades.

Cork's approach is not the Ashbourne or Red Rox model, with a focus on youth. Instead, it's people from many different countries looking for an outlet to play baseball. From that base, they seem to want to introduce baseball to the rest of Cork through the enthusiasm they have for the game. Maybe at some stage that will include youth baseball and development of that kind. But for right now, it's just a different focus. Still, for all of these differences, what all of the teams I've seen so far do have in common is an emphasis on positivity, fun, and community. Everyone seems to realize that baseball, played like it is here at a grassroots level, is not guaranteed to survive and that means it needs to be a fun activity for both kids and adults. It needs to be a supportive community, a group of people others are going to want to spend time with. It needs to be about competition and individual improvement, but it also has to be enjoyable. Whatever their differences, the people running the show in Cork and at the various clubs in Dublin all understand those underlying principles.

DUBLIN

It's such an experience, playing in the rain and bad weather and soggy balls and the mud. That's how much we love the game, you know.

—DANIEL "WOODY" WOODBURNE, MARINERS BASEBALL

SATURDAY, JULY 1, 2023

I'm back on the train to Shankill for a game between the Mariners and the Renegades. The ride is much shorter today as we're staying in Booterstown, one of Dublin's coastal suburbs. It's a pleasant walk from the station in the Saturday morning sunshine; the trek is much shorter now that I know where the ballfield is located in the immensity of Shanganagh Park. Both teams are already there getting their equipment organized, stretching, and readying themselves for the game. Some of the Mariners are nearly finished attaching the bottom netting behind home plate. The left- and right-field lines are freshly painted, as are the out-of-bounds lines a few yards beyond. Runners get one extra base on hits that go past these lines, while catches made out of bounds are not counted as outs since those spaces would be beyond a fence if the field were permanent, as it is in Ashbourne or at Corkagh Park.

I see Shan from Connecticut, ask him how he likes being back playing baseball. "My mind is loving it," he replies, "but my body is hating it. People at work ask me, 'What's wrong with you?' I tell them, 'Baseball.'" He laughs as he continues to lace up his cleats, but I note the slight grimace when he rises from the grass.

A few of the Renegades call out as I make my way over to where they have decamped on the first-base side of the field. Filip grins and says hello. Matt takes a pull on his vape, then laughs and tells me that I must be good luck for the weather. I ask him how his ribs feel. Still sore is the verdict. Kai and Mihnea Dragan play catch towards the outfield. Andrés is in conversation with Alejandro, perhaps going over the lineup for today's game. Later that afternoon, Alejandro will tell me that he grew up in the shadow of the Caracas Lions stadium and that he's been in love with baseball for his entire life. As he puts it, "In baseball, you always learn something new."

Behind the backstop, I notice a young man watching the teams warming up, and eventually I overhear that his name is James. I wonder if it's James Kelly, the pitcher who was named MVP at the European Cup Qualifier that the Mariners won last weekend, beating Sundbybergs BSC from Sweden by a score of 5–2 in the championship game. Kelly pitched the final five innings of that game, giving up just three hits and a walk, and no runs. At seventeen, he's one of the rising stars of the Irish youth program, someone Jason Wiebe suggested I speak with.

I introduce myself then ask him if he is James Kelly. He confirms that he is. Before I can begin to ask him questions, however, a lanky man clad in baseball pants, stirrup socks, a white-and-blue half-sleeve T-shirt, a Mariners cap, and glasses ambles over, cleats in hand, to speak with James about the game. Today is the first game that James will umpire, as he is newly slotted into the rotation of players that every club needs to make available to the league. Paddy

Flemming, though playing today, is an experienced umpire, one of three or four in the country who works every weekend. He just got back from umpiring at the European Cup Qualifier and has also previously worked at other European Qualifying tournaments. He'll be the plate umpire for the second game today, between the Red Rox and the Vikings, another of the Mariners' B teams, but right now he wants to give James some pointers about where to position himself in the field as he umps his first game.

As Paddy walks back to the Mariners' bench, I ask James about his background in baseball. He tells me that he has been playing for twelve years, beginning at the age of five when he lived in New Jersey. Originally from Australia, from the US his family moved to Singapore, where he played even more baseball. They eventually settled in Ireland in 2019, when James was thirteen. A left-handed pitcher, he began playing for the Mariners and last year was the main starter for the Vikings. This year he has moved up to mainly playing in the A League, impressing the Mariners so much that they relied on him as one of their staff for the tournament in Sweden. He didn't disappoint.

James quickly shifts the conversation towards Strike Zone, where you can find him at least three times per week. He tells me that he's seen "crazy improvements" this offseason and that "Frank is a massive help." He goes on to talk about how he has been able to develop velocity with control and how Frank has been able to help him to think about what he calls "pitch craft." But it's not just Frank, it's also the group of players who train together at the facility: "Everyone's there, and they're all determined to get better. It's a good group." When I ask him why baseball, he replies, "It's a team—you're with all your friends, I guess, and you're practising together. I've always enjoyed that—working with a group of people you get to know well. There's lots of time to talk and have fun, but it's also competing—that brings a strong bond." With one year of high school remaining, James is one of the next crop of players who hope to play college baseball in the US. He's seen what this year's group did in the recruitment process and understands that this summer he needs to put together his own video to send out to coaches if he wants to follow in their footsteps.

The Mariners take the field. James Thornton at first, Mike Mohler at second, Paddy Flemming at short, and Shan Momi at third. As they take grounders, I talk with a player from the Renegades who joined the conversation I was having with James Kelly when we were discussing the young players coming up through the system. His hair is close-cropped, and there are laugh lines around his eyes. He tells me that he is originally from Pittsburgh and is also named James Kelly. James Kelly the Elder. In his forties, he plays not only for the Renegades, but also for the Mariners' A team, who play tomorrow at Corkagh Park. He'll also be the field umpire for today's second game. When I ask him about umpiring, he tells me, "You have to pay attention to completely different things." What he will make for today's second game will just about pay for his gas from Cork; crashing at a friend's place means he can get in a full weekend of baseball without breaking the bank.

A few minutes later, the home plate umpire calls for the Mariners' starter to throw his final two warmup pitches. James the Elder strides to the plate and sets himself, ready for the first pitch of the game. From the Renegades' bench, Alec yells, "Give 'em the Pittsburgh special!" On the next pitch, James singles up the middle, under the glove of the second baseman. After he takes second on a wild pitch, time is called because people are walking their dogs across the outfield. Filip then steps back into the batter's box and hammers the first pitch for a ground-rule double into the uncut grass in left field. 1–0 Renegades. Andrés comes up and hits the ball into almost exactly the same section of grass for another ground-rule double. 2–0 Renegades. I hear James telling a teammate what the fastball and curve look like out of the pitcher's hand. Single and another run scores. 3–0 Renegades. But that's it for runs, thanks in part to a great play to get the force at second for out number two, Mike ranging to his right and making it to the bag before the runner. Andrés comes out to pitch for the Renegades and sets the Mariners down in order. 3–0 at the end of the first.

There are runners on the corners, and it's already 7–0 in the second inning. From the Mariners' bench I hear someone yell to the pitcher, "Short memory. This is what you focus on. Attack that zone." Despite a balk, only one more run scores. From the Renegades' bench I hear Matt chanting, "Nicotine. Nicotine. Nicotine. That's my game day vape."

A few more people have stopped to watch, swelling the crowd to perhaps fifteen people, a combination of family, friends, and onlookers who have stumbled upon the game. A couple of kids in GAA shirts stand on the first-base side discussing the rules. An older couple walking their dog stops behind home plate and watches for a few minutes. A father and son carrying hurleys have to stop briefly when their dog runs onto the field of play. Behind the Renegades' bench, James explains to the couple and their daughter that it is a proper match. The woman tells him it's the first time she's seen baseball live. The inning chugs along, the Renegades scoring an additional five runs to make it 13–0.

The Mariners' half of the third opens with six consecutive walks, followed by two doubles. At one point, Filip throws the ball on a line from left field to hold a runner at third, but it only briefly holds back the onslaught. In the blink of an eye, the score is 13–7. A passed ball makes it 13–8 before two more walks load the bases again. Andrés can no longer throw strikes—almost everything is high, and what's not is getting hammered by the Mariners. As manager, he's left himself in too long. Finally, he signals for Alec to come in and relieve him. Alec throws mostly junk, fairly slow pitches with lots of movement, the ball looping out of his hand as it comes towards the hitter. When he strikes out the first batter he faces, I think that maybe he'll be able to fool the Mariners' hitters and get the Renegades out of the inning. But he can't and he doesn't. By the time the inning ends, the Mariners have erased the Renegades' thirteen-run lead and now lead 19–13.

The Red Rox team are warming up to the right of the outfield. I check the time on my phone and see that the current game is not going to go seven innings—they'll be lucky to get in five before the next game needs to start. I keep one eye on the field and the other on the players in bright red jerseys tossing balls to each other in preparation for their upcoming game. Sometime during the fourth inning, Eric Bentley, the father of James, one of the Red Rox players, sidles up to me. He reminds me that we met briefly at Strike Zone when he was dropping his son off last week. I ask how James got into baseball, and he tells me that Frank came to his school to do a demonstration. When James came home that day, he was talking about dingers. Eric tells me that he turned to his wife and said, "What's that? Drugs, is it?" He laughs. Neither of them had a clue about the sport, but James took to it immediately, dropping hurling and focusing instead on baseball. Eric maintains that baseball is a sport to which hurlers are suited and that making the transition to a sport with much less competition for playing time would be beneficial to them. It's one of the first conversations I've had about kids moving from one sport to another. As we talk, the fourth inning comes to an end. I've lost track of the score and have to ask Alejandro. 22–14 Mariners.

The Renegades come to the plate and begin to make up the deficit through a combination of walks, steals, and wild pitches. A woman behind us walks up and says, "My mam and myself are cudgeling our brains over there, wondering why they're not hitting the ball. Is the ball too low?" I explain how the strike zone works, wondering to myself if I've ever seen this many walks in a game. As I watch the inning continue to unfold, I talk with Todd Westover, who has two sons playing for the Red Rox. As he explains that his wife works for Kellogg's and is on assignment in Dublin for three years, I hear the familiar flat vowels of Michigan. Baseball and the Red Rox have represented an important transition for not only the kids, but for the family as a whole, and as he speaks, I begin to see the admiration he has for baseball as it is played here.

"It's about playing all the kids. It's about getting them engaged so they stay with it, right, and become the next generation of coaches, versus winning at all costs." Baseball Ireland is, in Todd's estimation, "doing it the right way" in trying to grow the game from the ground up. "In the States, kids get out of baseball at thirteen. Here they're starting at eleven, twelve, and it's more of a lifelong thing." He goes on to speak glowingly of Juan Lucas Galan and the countless hours he puts in coaching. "All the stuff falls on just a couple of guys here." He's talking about the Red Rox, but he could be talking about any of the clubs here.

Meanwhile, there are more walks and a few key hits. By the time the top of the inning ends, the score is 25–22 Renegades, heading into the bottom of the fifth and final inning of play. When Shaun Grant told me that "it's a high-scoring environment," he wasn't kidding.

Alec gets a quick K to start the frame, but after a couple of singles, a pair of walks, a hit batter, and an error, the score is tied at 25 with the bases loaded. Fittingly, the winning run comes home on a walk. A walk-off, 26–25 win for the Mariners. Elvis has finally left the building.

SUNDAY, JULY 2, 2023

Jason Wiebe pulls his car into the parking lot of the Booterstown DART station. I push off the wall I'm leaning against, nod in acknowledgement, and open the car door. We're off to Corkagh Park for today's A League game between the Giants and the Dublin Spartans, but first we'll swing by Jason's house to pick up Ryan. I'm grateful for the ride, as Corkagh is almost impossible to access via public transportation. The Sunday transit schedule will mean that I must leave before the start of the Mariners–Hurricanes game, and even then I will only be able to make it back to city centre and eventually our flat by hitching a ride with Sean Mitchell to the Red Cow LUAS station.

As we drive through the south suburbs of Dublin, I think about how different my experience of the city has been this trip. I had been to Dublin many times before, but this trip is making me realize that my internal map of the city extended only a few blocks past the Liffey to the Gate Theatre in the north to a few blocks past the Grand Canal in the south, and from Dublin Bay in the east to Kilmainham Gaol in the west. There is no baseball in this part of Dublin, and in chasing baseball here, my mental construct of the city has expanded to include Finglas, Glasnevin, Phibsborough, Ashbourne, Portmarnock, Booterstown, Shankill, and Corkagh. The city of those who live here, rather than the city of those who only visit.

We stop to pick up Ryan, drinking coffee as we wait for him to finish getting ready. I ask Jason about the Giants team we'll see today, and he tells me that it will mostly be young guys who have come up through the system. He goes on to say that "the top players coming out of the Academy program are now among the top players in the A League." These players want to play as much as possible and could play several times a week since they don't have the work or family commitments of the older players. For now, there does not seem to be enough of a groundswell for the schedule to move beyond one game per week, but Jason thinks this will change in the near future. "Five years from now, when the Academy program has produced that many more players, I think we'll start to have the A League transitioning to play twice a week or something like that."

This question of how many games to play each week seems, on the surface, to be of little consequence, but at the heart of this tension are differences that are both generational and reflections of what individual players want from league play. I was more than a bit surprised when I first saw that I would have to plan the entire itinerary—with the exception of the BBF tournament in Slough—around the rhythm of a game on the weekend and a training session during the week. In watching baseball in southern Ontario and in Michigan over the last twenty years and in the course of the research for *100 Miles of Baseball*, I had become accustomed to virtually all teams playing multiple games per week, whether they were in amateur, high school, collegiate, minor, or major leagues. What was different here? As

I listened to Jason speak, it struck me that players in these North American leagues are often striving to get to the next level or, if they are at the top of the amateur or pro tiers, to stay at that level. Here and in the other places I will visit, there is, or has been, almost no room to move to the next level. The game is about competition, yes, but more than that, it's about fun and community and a good day out. This is grassroots baseball, the soil from which the game has grown in Ireland. But now—particularly because of Strike Zone—there is a group of young players who *do* want to get to the next level. And they see the next level as not only the National Team, but collegiate baseball in the US. These players want different things out of baseball than most of the older or more social players, a tension that needs to be managed intelligently in order to sustain an ecosystem in which the game can grow without alienating existing players.

We park in a residential neighbourhood on the verge of Corkagh Demesne Park and walk along a paved trail towards the National Baseball Facility, a small part of the much larger park, unknown to all but those directly involved in baseball in Ireland. A faded wooden sign points ahead towards *Fairywood*, *Baseball Playing Fields*, and *Arboretum*. Jason points out the stone commemorating the opening of the park. It's badly worn, and I have to strain to make out the words: *O'Malley Little League and Dodger Baseball Fields*. Open since 1998, the two fields—Little League to the left and the larger field to the right—were funded by Peter O'Malley, owner of the Los Angeles Dodgers. Outside of the International Baseball Centre in Ashbourne, it is still the only permanent diamond in the country. It's no wonder that the 10 x 10 plan foregrounds the need for facilities.

The field is a beautiful expanse of green, ringed by hedges all around the outfield, an outer boundary that replaces the wall seen in most parks in North America; balls that roll into the hedge go for a ground-rule double. Beyond those hedges is a stand of trees that forms a break between the field and the houses beyond. From right field, I see a beautiful diamond carved into the field, with a permanent mound and dirt basepaths. Behind home plate is a permanent backstop, and along the first and third baselines are team benches that sit behind protective fencing. A couple of the Spartans are raking the dirt around home, but there's none of the preparatory work I saw yesterday at Shanganagh.

I watch the Spartans set up for batting practice, and I hear one of them say, "It's just because we haven't played in three weeks that my body feels okay." Unlike the Giants, the Spartans' team is comprised mainly of players who are thirty years or older, though there are a couple of exceptions, one of whom is David Casey. While he came up through the Ashbourne organization, he's pitching for the Spartans this summer as a way to get in more innings. He's one of ten players out today for the Spartans, the same number that the Giants have available.

Sean Mitchell has just arrived, setting up his lawn chair on the berm to the first-base side of home plate. He's been cajoled into keeping score for the Giants today and is in the process of entering the starting lineup into his scorebook. Feidhlim Deering, who I saw pitch last weekend for the Giants' B team, is on the mound to start. With him now as he warms up is his battery mate, Fionn Gallahar-Hall, who will also act as manager for the team today. I recognize a number of the young Giants standing near their dugout—Ryan Wiebe, David Linn, Patrick Mitchell, Miguel Ascensio. Of today's players, the only one over twenty-three is Miguel

Moreno, who will play third base and bat fifth. Sean points out David McCarthy, who will be playing on the U18 team this year, and then gestures at Damian and Ronan Pruszkowski, brothers who originally hail from South Africa. Damian's pants are several sizes too big for him, a detail that Sean, Jason, and I all notice simultaneously.

Feidhlim and Fionn return to the bench, and Fionn proceeds with his pre-game talk. "Start playing as a team. Every pitch, every at bat. Cheer each other on. Play as a team and pick each other up." Fionn's talk ends, and the team cheers in unison as they get ready to take the field. But before they leave the dugout, someone says to Damian, "You need suspenders, man." Damian replies, "Yeah, Jason just needs to buy me new pants." Jason just rolls his eyes, muttering under his breath. He plasters a smile to his face and yells back, "You have to let us know if your pants don't fit." Sean just laughs and continues to ready his scorecard.

Clad in their brown jerseys with the word *Ashbourne* in orange lettering across their chests and caps with a simple block *A*, the Giants take their places on the field. But previous rainouts and scheduling issues have caused there to be some confusion over who is supposed to be the home team. After some discussion, it's determined that the Spartans are actually home. As the Giants leave the field, one of the Spartans shouts, "Good inning, boys!"

Pitching for the Spartans today is Brendan Scott, a righthanded stalwart of the Spartans' staff and long-time member of the National Team. Hands together just below his bearded face, he quickly raises his front leg and strides towards the plate with his last warmup toss. The home plate umpire motions for David Linn, the Giants' leadoff hitter. He settles into the box and works a walk to start the game. After Ryan hits into a fielder's choice, Fionn laces a ball to right field that rolls into the hedge for a ground-rule double. With runners on the corners, Patrick hits a sacrifice fly to score one, with a second run coming in on an overthrow to third. A ground ball to short ends the inning. 2–0 Giants.

The Giants replace the Spartans in the field. Behind Feidhlim, Damian is at first base, David McCarthy at second, Miguel at third, and Patrick at short. The outfield, from left to right, consists of David Linn, Ryan, and Ronan. Feidhlim doesn't have excessive velocity, but his breaking ball seems to fool the Spartan hitters, inducing soft contact rather than the strikeouts that it did in the early innings against the Renegades last weekend. The pitch breaks like a slider, though when I ask him about it, Feidhlim calls it a curve. Whatever it is, the pitch yields two groundouts to third to open the inning. He gives up a ground-rule double into the hedge in right field, but a weak tapper back to the pitcher strands the runner on second. 2–0 Giants.

With a man on in the second, Damian hits a bloop single just over first base as one of his teammates yells, "Way to keep your pants on!" Scott walks behind the mound and settles himself before stepping back on the rubber and striking out the next two hitters. That brings up David Linn, who reaches base on a routine ground ball that the third baseman can't handle. In the ensuing confusion, Feidhlim, the lead runner, tries to take home, but is thrown out at the plate. For the moment, the score remains unchanged. In the bottom of the inning, however, the Spartans score five, all unearned, to make the score 5–2 Spartans.

Ryan leads off the third inning with a single on a very bad hop after it hits a rock near second base. Sean looks up from his scorecard and shouts, "Corkagh bounce. Way to play the geography!" while from the bench I hear David Linn comment, "This field wants errors." The Giants score two but leave the bases loaded. In the bottom half of the inning, Patrick makes a great play at shortstop, diving to his right before popping up and throwing a laser to first base for the out. The Spartans' inning ends on a fly ball to right field just as the sun disappears and the rain begins. One of the parents comments, "All seasons in two minutes."

From the Giants' bench someone asks Sean, "Who's up?"

"Top of the shop," he replies. I've never before heard this phrase, so it takes me a second to realize that he means top of the order. Patrick is throwing in foul territory past first base, getting ready to take over from Feidhlim in the bottom of the inning. But when Ryan reaches base, he has to halt his warmup to take his place in the on-deck circle. By the time he comes in to pitch, the score is 6–5 Giants.

Patrick is tall and slender like his father, and you can tell by watching him—whether taking grounder, on the mound, or in the batter's box—that he has grown up around baseball. You see the muscle memory that can't really be developed in adults who learn the game, the way of carrying himself on the field. He has a certain swagger, a confidence in his own abilities that's especially evident when he takes the mound. A right-hander, Patrick throws harder than anyone I've yet seen on this trip—likely somewhere in the high 80s. As he strides to the plate and releases the ball, the white chain he wears around his neck flicks upward before settling back on his jersey. It's an explosive step, his trailing leg whipping behind him, finishing high and pulling him slightly toward first base. There's definite life on the fastball, the primary pitch he uses in striking out the first two Spartan hitters. But then a walk and a single score the tying run, while an error plates the go-ahead run for the Spartans. Another walk—this time to David Casey—and a stolen base put runners on second and third. To my right,

I hear Sean shouting in Irish, encouraging Patrick as he takes a deep breath and walks back to the mound. Strikeout looking. 7–6 Spartans. As the Giants come to their bench, I hear Miguel encouraging his young teammates: "That's the good of baseball. You have many chances."

The Giants fail to score in the top of the fifth, and Patrick takes the bump again for the bottom of the inning. A walk and a steal put a man on second. Called third strike for out number one, a call the batter vociferously disputes, drawing a line in the dirt with his bat. He's still jawing with the home plate umpire when Paddy Flemming, the field umpire, decisively tosses him out of the game. The runner moves up on a ground ball to third, but is stranded when Miguel Moreno makes a great play, sweeping his glove up in an arc and somehow managing to nab a hot grounder and throw out the batter at first. It's still a one-run game going into the sixth inning.

In the top of the sixth, the Giants score a run before Patrick doubles to score two more for a 9–7 lead. The Spartans come back with a run in the bottom half of the inning. No runs in the seventh, and as we come to the top of the eighth, the score is 9–8 Giants.

A single to put runners at the corners finally chases Brendan Scott from the game after 130 pitches. David Casey in to pitch. He begins with his left foot slightly in front of his right. He then pushes off, his right leg swinging around towards first base on the follow through. He gives up a single to score one before getting a fly ball for out number two. A base knock from Damian loads the bases, bringing up Miguel Ascensio to pinch hit. Infield single and the bases are loaded again. Miguel's mother and father are here once again, her clapping and cheering, him nodding along to Miguel's play. With David McCarthy at the plate, Miguel Moreno steals home, putting the Giants up 12–8.

Damian comes in to pitch in the bottom of the eighth inning, setting the Spartans down in order. Most of the Mariners and Hurricanes have arrived for the next game. Some stretch, some toss the ball. Others watch the game. I introduce myself to Daniel Woodburne, one of the Mariners' players I had been in contact with before the trip. I ask him about the experience of playing in the tournament in Sweden, and he replies, "We were looking to get one win. That was the goal. And the fact that we won the tournament was huge. We wanted to send a statement out—with us local guys, that we could play ball, that we could compete. We kept it local, and we actually won." Throughout our conversation, he keeps coming back to the idea of developing local players and not relying on imports, both at the club level and for the National Team. At one point, someone on the edge of our conversation mentions the group from the US who are lobbying for the Irish National Team to include more passport holders, essentially adopting the strategy that Great Britain used to get to the World Baseball Classic. As with everyone else when this topic comes up, Daniel grimaces and explains why this approach is a bad idea and how it actually works against growing the game here. He tells me about friends of his who play with the London Mets. Despite performing at a very high level in league play, none of these players have any real shot at playing on the Great Britain team because of their reliance on players from the US. Daniel says, "I'd rather win the C pool [rather than the A pool in which Great Britain competes] organically with local guys and have the same guys play and develop the game, the league, and the country." It's the same philosophy that lies behind the 10 x 10 plan.

I ask him about James Kelly, and Daniel's face lights up. "What a performance! ERA of 0. Ten innings he pitched, more than ten strikeouts." He also speaks highly of Patrick Mitchell's performance: "He's a rocket fire. He was bringing it in Sweden as well. He's just so dominant as a pitcher. He's really the future of baseball in Ireland." And yet, despite his talk about what James and Patrick did, Daniel was the one who won the pitching award for the tournament. When I bring it up, Daniel says, "Just when I thought I was going to hang up my cleats. Baseball has an amazing way of giving back."

Daniel is constantly greeting players from every team, laughing and smiling, clearly at ease at the ballpark, a place that's been his home for nearly thirty years. He started playing when he was eight and living in Belgium, moving to Ireland in 2004 with his Irish parents when he was eighteen. Upon discovering baseball in Ireland, he chose to take up his Irish passport and began playing for the National Team, where he remained for the next fifteen years. He's been playing with the Mariners since 2015. It still captures his imagination, still feels like fun. "Baseball," Daniel tells me, "has been my life."

As we talk, the game proceeds, the Giants tacking on four more runs in the top of the ninth. What was a very close game for most of the way ends with the Giants winning 16–8. In the changeover between games, there is a lot of mingling of jerseys as players from the different teams greet each other, shaking hands or bumping fists. There is much laughter, and the overlapping conversations are almost overwhelming. Though I've seen intense competition on the diamond these past two weeks, there is also a sense of camaraderie, a community of baseball that transcends individual teams. There are, of course, disagreements and grudges, stuck as they are with each other in this small community. But, for better or worse, there's also a sense that in playing this niche, grassroots sport, they are all in it together, playing the game they love. Playing Irish baseball.

ABERDEEN

> My dad played; he passed away when I was really young. I'm not sure which position, but I know he played baseball. My aunt played baseball—she was an umpire as well. My cousins all played. I love it—can't get enough of it. I'm rubbish at it, but I love it.
>
> —CASEY MACKENZIE, MANAGER, GRANITE CITY OILERS

TUESDAY, JULY 4, 2023

I pull my jacket close against the wind blowing off the North Sea. Early July in Aberdeen. Fifteen degrees and the heat of Dublin only a memory. Across the marsh and out into the sea loom the row of wind turbines, eleven of them strung across the horizon. Waves break against the shore, lapping sand that will become rock when we make the turn south from the River Don, headed for City Beach. I stop and stare across the water toward Norway and Denmark, enthralled by the rough beauty of the waves, as I am already by Aberdeen itself.

It was overcast when we arrived yesterday from Dublin, the mechanics of travel a numbing interlude between segments of the trip. With no training to attend until tomorrow, I've done nothing but walk the city—from our flat at Park Place to the University of Aberdeen and Seaton Park, to the River Don, to Footdee and city centre and Torry. It's often called Granite City, a name that makes sense as you meander the streets, nearly every building grey on its face. At first glance, the city is almost dour, and certainly outwardly serious. Stolid. But as you walk, you also see the pops of colour in the street art. You turn a corner and see a rainbow of brightly coloured umbrellas suspended above a street in city centre, a way to raise awareness of neurodiversity in Scotland. And the weather is often grey, as it was on the day we arrived, but when the sun pokes through the clouds, it glints off the buildings' granite faces, showing them in such beautiful definition.

There's a hard surface to the city, but underneath is something beautiful. It's an unforgiving locale here by the North Sea—bracingly cold even on a summer's day like today—and maybe Aberdeen itself needs to have that kind of granite solidity against those adverse conditions. But from it comes a craggy kind of beauty, rough and wondrous as the sea itself.

WEDNESDAY, JULY 5, 2023

The sun comes out for the first time today as I leave the flat. Tonight I'm attending training for the Granite City Oilers, one of six teams in Baseball Scotland's AAA, or highest, division. Four teams comprise the A division, all of whom are affiliated with an organization that also fields an AAA team. Established in 2013, the Aberdeen Baseball Club at one time also included the Aberdeen Express, and it has occasionally fielded a women's team called the Aberdeen Thistles. But, according to Casey Mackenzie, the manager of the Oilers, between COVID and players leaving Aberdeen, the team is currently struggling to pull together enough players for even one team. Tonight I'll meet the few who remain.

I close the door to the flat and trace a path towards the sea. Just before I get to the entrance to the park, I veer north, up the hill that overlooks the green and beyond it, the North Sea. The face of the hill is rough grass dotted with thistle, purple bursts of colour in a sea of green. In the corner of the park closest to the hill, I can see the outlines of the diamond far below, cutouts for the bases, a rough mound, and a permanent home plate. The park itself is a massive square bordered on the west by the hill on which I'm standing, on the north by a driving range, on the south by Linx Ice Arena, and on the east by the North Sea. Past the diamond within the park is a cricket pitch. There's a lot of space here, but it's shared by multiple teams and individual users, a situation that is not always amicable.

As I wait for the players to arrive, I wander towards the berm that separates the field from the road that runs along the sea. Standing at its apex, I marvel at the quality of midsummer light as it glints across the water before glancing back over my shoulder to see if anyone has arrived yet. From the far northwest corner of the park, from beyond what would be left field foul territory, I see someone pulling a cart laden with what must be baseball equipment. I hurry down the hill and across the park, arriving at the same time as a young man somewhere in his early twenties, with close-cropped hair and thick glasses, dressed in full baseball uniform. Grey pants. Red socks, high to the knee. Umbro cleats. Dark blue jersey with *OILERS* in red script outlined in white emblazoned across his chest. Cap crested with an *A* in matching colours. His name is Jackson McGregor, and he tells me that he's often the first one here, bringing in the equipment from their storage locker near the parking lot and setting everything up. As we talk, he empties the cart, anchors bases in their holes in the centre of the cutouts, and erects the net they will use as a makeshift backstop. As he fits the base at second, he yells to someone sitting on the cricket pitch that they will be training tonight. "It's very unusual," Jackson says, "for us to have a good day like this for baseball."

Jackson tells me that he's been playing for about two and a half years and is learning both the catcher and pitcher positions, partly from other players and partly through tutorials on YouTube. I ask him about how he got into baseball, and he tells me that he stumbled by the pitch one night when he was drunk and that's how he found out there was baseball here. Later that evening, Casey tells me the same story about how Jackson came to the game and to the Oilers. He had tried many sports over the years, but baseball was the sport that stuck, even though he had to learn it from scratch as an adult. Of Jackson, Casey tells me, "He's calmed down a lot more. He's got really bad ADHD. And this gives him a purpose [...]. If I can help other people control ADHD or anything like that by including them in things they wouldn't have had before, I'll keep doing it." Baseball, Jackson says, provides "a sense of relief for me" and "gets me through a lot of things."

Casey and her daughter Erin arrive carrying a bag of balls and bats. Like Jackson, Casey is in full uniform, though her pants cover any hint of sock and a ponytail sprouts from the back of her faded cap. Ex-military, Casey moved back home to Aberdeen at the end of her time in the service, but the return to civilian life was a shock, especially in a city where she no longer knew many people. "There was an aloneness—people around, but nothing I belonged to anymore." It was because of Erin that Casey came to the Oilers, though she thought at the time that it would just be another sport that Erin tried and gave up. That was in 2018. Not only are they still coming, but Casey has become the main driving force behind the Oilers.

I ask Erin what it was about baseball that was different from other sports. She replies, "It's the feeling it gives me. I don't know how to describe it. It's just good. It's a part of my life, and it feels like when I started playing baseball, something totally shifted in my body." As she speaks, I think of how similar her answer is to what David Linn and Kai Gao told me when I asked the same question. *I can't put it into words; I just know how it feels.* She goes on to talk about how she also wanted to be part of something, to belong to a community of people who felt like she did about the game. Five years in and she's still excited to play, a turn of events that Casey never expected, but one she welcomed, especially as she herself got further enmeshed in the team. It started with helping to coach the kids and then helping out on game days with the adult team, which led into umpiring, even though she freely admits that she doesn't know all the rules. Needs must. Or, as Casey says, "We all do what we need to do."

From umpiring, she moved to playing, and when much of the team disappeared around the time of COVID, she stepped in to keep the team going. "When all the coaches left the adult team, someone had to step up. I was the only one left to take over the team." It is, as she terms it, "a big rebuild," with a large number of the current players having only played a year or so, some coming straight to the Oilers and some—like Subin and Clemence, who are here tonight—having played initially with the Aberdeen University Baseball Club. In the current group of players there are people from Scotland, Canada, Venezuela, Greece, Italy, and Nepal. "Everyone [on the team] was really welcoming," Casey tells me, "and I've tried to keep that with everyone gone and new people coming in. I've tried to make it as welcoming and friendly as possible." It is clear that Casey sees the team as a community first—a way to work against the isolation that too many people feel for too many different reasons—and that community has to be the basis for building the team. As we talk, I keep coming back to Sean Mitchell's idea that every team needs to have a driving force on the ground. In Aberdeen, that is clearly Casey Mackenzie.

Players continue to filter in to the diamond, some pairing off to play catch while others take the opportunity to stretch and catch up with teammates. A family on vacation from Houston arrives, the mother is originally from Aberdeen, the father originally from Leeds. The boys, aged ten and thirteen, were born and raised in America, and they both play travel baseball. The parents have arranged for the boys to train with the team tonight in lieu of the practices and games they're missing at home. Perhaps an enticement to make the weeks in the UK more palatable. I watch them warm up, first playing catch and then throwing ground balls to each other. No doubt they've played some ball. As I watch the older boy square to a ground ball, I hear a Scottish accent behind me proclaim, "José Altuve is the only reason I play baseball."

By the time everyone arrives, there are fifteen people ready to play. They begin by doing some group stretching and a bit of light running. Since they have enough players for a game, there will be no drills tonight—the feeling is that with so many players new to baseball, what they really need are actual game situations. They quickly divide into two teams with Casey on one side and Erin on the other. The boys from Houston are on opposing teams, a little friendly rivalry between brothers. Casey's team takes the field as the other side quickly puts together a batting order.

Just beyond right field, twenty football players run wind sprints, sometimes drifting on to what will be the field of play. The Oilers pay to use the facility for training and for games, despite their low numbers, while other teams—like this football team—show up without booking or paying. And even though it's not perfect, this field is under threat from more than just other sports, as it's scheduled to become a parking lot in the near future. In the plans for the new field, the place of the Oilers is precarious. For the Oilers, as for the Renegades in Cork, finding a venue at which to train and play is the top priority. And, as in Cork, the solution is not readily apparent. Throughout my travels, the issue of securing a stable place to play is an ongoing theme.

Next to me, a preteen girl talks on the phone: "I'm outside by the field. Mom's doing baseball." Joanna, her mother, is originally from Venezuela. She played growing up and then played on a women's team in the Netherlands. As Joanna waits to bat, she tells me that she plays with whatever team is around wherever she is living and that she just recently moved to Aberdeen. Immediately after she tells me this, she singles through the hole between second and third. Not long after, play is halted briefly when the ball gets lost in the tall grass behind home plate.

There are some good swings and a handful of decent plays in the field, but it isn't well-played baseball by any stretch of the imagination. The younger Texan has a good fastball for his age, even managing to strike out his brother, a feat that will, I'm sure, live on well past their vacation. Casey strikes out Erin, which elicits a sly grin from Casey and an incredulous "Mom!" from Erin. Later Casey will tell me, "Today's the first day I've managed to participate in the actually playing—the training itself." The numbers tonight and the ensuing game have allowed it. It's a fun night for the players with lots of laughter and camaraderie, but it is, overall, a different level and kind of baseball than I saw in Ireland or that I would see at home. This is baseball played mainly by adults who are new or relatively new to the game. It makes me realize yet again that baseball is, and represents, different things to different people.

By mutual agreement, the game comes to an end, though I have no idea who won or what the score was. That was never really the point. Being with other people, out in the sun, laughing, playing baseball near the North Sea on a beautifully sunny night in early July: that was the point. After the session, the boys' mother tells me that they told her "the reason they'd never move to the UK is there's no baseball here. We just proved them wrong." I wonder if those two kids from Houston have grins as big as they did tonight when they play travel baseball in Texas.

It would have been easy to watch training tonight and write it off, just as it would be easy to see Aberdeen as grey and imposing. But in both cases, it pays to look more closely, to see the beauty underneath the surface, to see what lies behind things as they are. There is, of course, something to striving to win and to pushing yourself at an individual level to be the best player you can be. But there's also something to using baseball as a way to move your body, to be with other people, to laugh. To find a slice of home, like James Kelly from the Renegades or Joanna here in Aberdeen, or to recapture one's youth, like the three American ex-pats from the Mariners. Or to grasp a way to fend off aloneness and find a sense of community, as Casey tries to nurture here in Aberdeen.

EDINBURGH

> It is a small sport, and because everyone loves the sport and everyone enjoys the social aspect as well, it's really good even just to come to practice.
>
> —CAITLIN MCCAFFREY,
> EDINBURGH DIAMOND DEVILS

THURSDAY, JULY 6, 2023

I watch the landscape tick past my window as we travel south on the train from Aberdeen to Edinburgh. Green and brown grass and scrub trees next to the sea. The occasional house set far from its neighbours. Fallow fields. Waves breaking against the rocky shore. Power lines bordering fields of ripening grain. Warehouses and greenhouses in the middle distance. The immense bridge across the Firth of Forth at Queensferry. Air travel may be efficient, but it is never relaxing—queues for check-in and security, navigating the airport to find your gate, manoeuvring to find a place to store your cabin bags. Train travel, on the other hand, acts as a pause, a space where time is suspended and your thoughts can drift with the passing landscape.

I put pen to paper, trying to get some of my thoughts down. *Baseball is baseball. But the baseball looks different here, looked different in Ireland. It's not only where they play, but how things are done and what people want out of the game. Against all odds. Precarious. Fragile, as Sean Mitchell put it. It's so much about belief from so many people and about a commitment to carve out spaces to play this game. Pulling together to keep things going. Who plays? Adults, yes. Kids, sometimes and in some places. Why do they play? What do they get out of the game? Community? Competition? Home? What am I seeing and why does it matter?*

I put down my pen and try to concentrate on the book I'm reading, but baseball, the specific baseball of this trip, keeps intruding. What started mainly as curiosity is becoming much more than that. As the train pulls in to Waverley Station, I wonder how Edinburgh—both tomorrow night's training and the game Sunday between the Diamond Devils and the Granite City Oilers—will fit into the fabric of my thoughts.

FRIDAY, JULY 7, 2023

Warriston Playing Fields. A wide space of green nestled between Howard Street, Eildon Street, and Warriston Crescent. In the far corner, opposite the entrance on Warriston Crescent, sits a squat white clubhouse covered in graffiti, tags both large and small. *MAD GORSE* in stylized lettering covers the end wall. Towering over this building, beyond the boundaries of the park, are long blocks of Edwardian flats. The sun shines on men and women in shorts and T-shirts playing catch in pairs. Watch for a few minutes and you can see that the majority of these players are not new to the game. Indistinct chatter mixes with the sound of ball hitting glove.

A temporary home plate faces away from the clubhouse, orienting play back towards the park's far entrance. Batting tees and nets are scattered in what would be foul territory. A lone young man in grey sweats and a blue Dodgers cap throws a hard rubber ball against one of the walls of the clubhouse, his target a smiley face with a crown above.

As training begins, I sit down with Caitlin McCaffrey, who has played for both the Edinburgh Diamond Devils and the club's A team, the Edinburgh Knights. She is currently injured, but she still attends training sessions. She is in her mid-to-late twenties, wears round glasses, sports shoulder-length blonde hair, and is quick to smile. Having just finished playing catch, she eases herself to the ground. At her feet sit a ball cap and glove. In the background, backing practice has commenced.

DJ. How long have you been playing baseball?

CAITLIN. I've actually only been playing baseball since August last year, but I used to play fastpitch.

DJ. Is fastpitch big here?

CAITLIN. Not really. Actually, slo-pitch here is quite a big thing. There's a huge league—I think there's fourteen teams that participate in slo-pitch, so it's much, much bigger than baseball here actually.

DJ. Right. So why did you switch from fastpitch?

CAITLIN. Honestly, it was just kind of a timing thing for me because I moved here mid-year last year from South Africa and I was looking to participate in a sport. The softball leagues are more kind of—they don't really do practising and stuff. It's more like they come during mid-week to play. I contacted one of the team members here off a Facebook post that they had made, and, yeah, they just said come down to practice. So I said great, and I've kind of been here ever since.

DJ. So, how is this? How is this team to play for?

CAITLIN. Oh, well, they're fantastic. I've played for both the Triple-A League, which is the higher league, the Diamond Devils. Unfortunately, this year they're having a bit of a tough year because we had a lot of changes on the team. So it's a very new team with regards to everyone playing together. Everyone's got a lot of skill, but we haven't played together as a team much. And then I've also played for the Single-A Edinburgh Knights. And they're fantastic. They're third at the moment in the league standings out of four, but hopefully after the Sunday game it'll be better. We'll probably be tied for second. Everyone's very encouraging, and it's a nice team—everyone's very social and quite happy to accept people coming in at any point during the season, which is nice.

DJ. It's kind of all different skill levels?

CAITLIN. Oh yes—you'll see. The other Triple-A team in Edinburgh is the Edinburgh Cannons, and they are the top of the league. A lot of the players here today are from the Cannons, and you'll see their skill level is very high. He's one of them that's just hit them all. [She points to a heavily muscled man taking batting practice.] The guys that are on the side of the field right now are all Cannons. And they are very, very skilled, and they will then teach the Knights, the Single-A players, some skills, and that's how we try and grow.

DJ. And then do the Knights feed into both those teams?

CAITLIN. Yeah, that's the idea. We do have a younger team—before the age of fourteen, you can play for the Edinburgh Giants. They're the young team, and then the idea is to bring up those players to the Knights and then from the Knights into either of the Triple-A teams.

DJ. So those fourteen and under, do they play in that Single-A league then?

CAITLIN. No, they don't. They just do a lot of practising and they play scrimmages amongst themselves. There's not really a league for that age group. Unfortunately, no, I don't think so. I don't think it's big enough.

DJ. One of the questions I've been asking people is what do your family and friends say when you say you're playing baseball?

CAITLIN. My family and friends keep telling me to stop because I keep injuring myself, but I think a lot of people kind of take baseball in Scotland as a bit of a joke, honestly, from what I've gathered here. Obviously coming from a different country, [my family doesn't] know what the perception of baseball is here, but I think generally from what I've heard, people, when you say—like when I say here at work that—I play baseball, people [there] are quite shocked [laughs] and [surprised] that it's actually a thing around Scotland. But I think now, with the London Series and stuff, that we've been actually doing quite well. In the leagues, hopefully we'll get a better image and people will get more involved.

DJ. Right. So the visibility has been pretty low?

CAITLIN. It's been a bit a low, but, I mean, you don't do it for the glory of, ohh wow, you're a baseball player! It's more for fun. Really. At this stage. So I don't really mind people looking at me funny.

DJ. So why baseball? Was it because mostly you played fastpitch and it was just the easiest transition?

CAITLIN. I think so. I'd moved here. I didn't have any friends or anyone, and I wanted to meet people and also get some exercise when I could. So that's why I thought, okay, well, I've played softball. How different could baseball be, really? So that was what it was for me. I could figure it out from my past experience.

DJ. And has it felt similar?

CAITLIN. It has felt very similar. It's just the whole batting situation is not my favourite because, as you can see, the ball does tend to come at you quite quickly. Softball, I mean it's fast, but it's not as intimidating as a man throwing like 60 plus miles per hour balls at your face, right? I think also because we do coed, it can be quite like intimidating. There are a few females—we've luckily managed to get more this year. I think last year [there was] Aska, and I think there was one other female. And this year we've got at least six, I think.

DJ. If you were talking to other people and trying to get them interested, what would you say? Why should they try baseball here?

CAITLIN. I've been trying to convince a lot of people at work to come and try it because, I mean, for me, it's fun. At the end of the day, it's fun. It's competitive, but not to the point of if you're losing, you feel bad about yourself. You'll see a lot of coaching happening, and if you make a mistake, your teammates are not berating you for that. It's very encouraging. I don't think anyone on this team or any of the three teams could say that they walked away from a game feeling bad about themselves.

Some players begin to line up for soft toss batting practice, while others wait to dig in against the pitching machine, its yellow dimpled balls almost as fast as any pitch they're likely to see in the league. Everyone else shags flies, hands on hips until a ball is in the air. A couple of players patrol the alleys between the bases, snagging the occasional ground ball, getting their reps in any way they can. One of the new players hits off a tee, while one of the more experienced players looks on and says, "Let the bat swing." Chatter and laughter echo around the park, providing the soundtrack of the evening.

I manage to corral Sylvain Morisot, player–manager for the Edinburgh Diamond Devils and my main contact in Edinburgh prior to coming to the park tonight. He is in his late thirties or early forties, slender, his features etched sharply on his face. His hair is short beneath his Diamond Devils cap.

DJ. So you're in the midst of trying to get a permanent field at this location?

SYLVAIN. Yeah, at this location we had a building permit a couple of years ago, just before COVID. And then, you know, it kind of stopped us in our tracks. And then after that, getting permission went off. And so now we're trying to see, but it's a little bit difficult. I'm not sure yet what the next step is for us in here, you know. Continue to train here? It's a beautiful location—you can see the Castle. Having to go off, getting a field maybe outside of Edinburgh—which would be easier to get a big space—that would be a shame because [there is] so much [foot] traffic here—the Botanic Garden right behind. People stand up with coffee and come and watch the field. So, it's a perfect location, but it's a little bit difficult. But if we ever do it our backstop would be by the swamp over there. [Points to the corner near the entrance on Warriston Avenue.] And we'll have the Green Monster with the tree in the outfield. [Points at the enormous elm at what would be the left-field corner.]

DJ. Gotcha. Yeah, that'd be great.

SYLVAIN. The field is actually not too bad. It's flat enough.

DJ. So are you hopeful that that's going to happen?

SYLVAIN. Yeah, I still have hope that we might get there. Either it's gonna happen in the next two years or it's never gonna happen. Right? At some point we [may] need to stop in our tracks and say, "Hey, what [should we] do?" Because it's not gonna happen here.

DJ. Are people surprised that there's baseball here?

SYLVAIN. Yeah, yeah, a lot of them are surprised. "Where? Where do you train? How do you get bats? How do you get balls?" With a lot of money. [He laughs long and hard.] It's a bit expensive to get here. Otherwise, people are quite supportive. It's pretty cool. And the only thing is if you're doing basketball, football, tennis, you get a lot of help, [but] if you're a minority sport, then it gets a little harder.

DJ. Is there anything like Sport Edinburgh or something that you are part of?

SYLVAIN. The problem is that a lot of us, we don't always have the time and the energy to write lengthy paperwork and forms and grants. If we had a few people who had the time to do it, we could definitely go further. If we had more time or people who had more time to go through that, then we probably get in a better position. I'm sure there are people who would be glad to help us, you know. So yeah, I think it's just that we need to find time.

DJ. That's the hard part, right?

SYLVAIN. Yeah, it's like everybody wants to play, but when it comes to organization, it's always a bit harder. And even though we get a lot of people, a lot of people you see here, half of them are just players who want to play. They don't mind helping with all the coaching and, you know, getting everything ready, mentoring all the other players. Even so, we don't have big infrastructures. Everybody is taking care of everyone in their own way. If you know a little bit more, you help someone.

DJ. Is it possible to get people interested in baseball?

SYLVAIN. Usually you're talking to fifty people before you get one. I would say seventy percent of people come and train here because they're either interested in baseball or have played before. A very small percentage are people to whom we've said, "Hey, come and train baseball." We get a lot of people here from South America or from the US—people who have played since they were kids and are here now for work or for studies. And a lot of the time they look for it. They say, "Hey, you know, I found you on Facebook or on Google. Can I come and try and play?" And we say, "Yeah, sure, no problem." But some people that we found over the years were like, "Wow, I've been in Edinburgh for seven years. I played baseball for so many years when I was a kid, and I'm only finding it now." So, we're not doing a good job—it's hard to get visibility for other people, so if people are not really looking for it, they're gonna miss it, right?

DJ. And the kids don't ever get it in schools or anything?

SYLVAIN. It's back to the same problem that was I explaining earlier. We need people who have time to go into schools. The schools are more than happy to include us, you know. I know a few schools that have P.E. teachers who played baseball in their youth. And once a month, they get a bunch of gloves and then they get the kids to do rounders and a right bit of baseball rules and history. So there is a way to do it, [but it means] having people who have time to be off work on mornings and during the week. So if we start to find these people, then that's definitely going to grow because as soon as you get people in schools then you see now the interest gets picked up.

DJ. But it's all volunteer, right? Baseball Scotland doesn't even have any paid employees?

SYLVAIN. No, no, no. All the money goes into buying baseballs and equipment and that sort of thing.

Steve Silverberg and Ryan MacFarlane have just finished throwing each other soft toss batting practice and are waiting for the evening's scrimmage to begin. Both play for the Cannons, while Ryan also manages the Knights in the A League. The two contrast each other: Steve is trimmer, has a narrow face with several days' growth, wears a Yankees cap, and speaks with a discernible New York accent. Ryan is a bit heavier set, with a round, clean-shaven face, and speaks with a pronounced Scottish accent.

DJ. So how long have you both been playing ball?

STEVE. I've been playing ball my whole life, since I was a kid, but I've only been here since—came and joined up with these guys in 2021. And then took a year hiatus back to the States, but now I'm here permanently. And yeah, it's great. I mean, I was shocked to find there was a league here when I moved, let alone one that [lets you] travel all over the country. Multiple teams in different cities.

DJ. It's been a good experience?

STEVE. It's been great! I thought my career was over, and it's been rejuvenated.

DJ. What about you? How long have you been playing?

RYAN. I've been on and off since probably about 2012. Played for a good couple of years and then took a break between university and stuff like that and then picked it back up. And then about five or six years ago again. So, a fair bit of time as well. But no, like Steve says, it's strange to find a league, especially with that many teams and now two leagues. One of the guys that I used to work with is one of the older players here, and he'd mentioned it and I just came down, tried it out and loved it and stayed here since.

DJ. What made you love it?

RYAN. I think it's just all the people here. It's a very come-together group as everybody gets on with everybody and all the teams are good together, even the same teams in the same cities, with the rivalries and stuff. Half the guys here are on the Devils, half on the Cannons.

DJ. What do co-workers or friends say when you say you're playing baseball here?

STEVE. I think they are excited by it. It's just such an unknown to so many people. Everybody has a different sense of what baseball is, and especially what baseball might be like here for people who don't know. But, to be honest, I think people would be shocked to come down and see it. It's such a well-organized league.

And I think a lot of people, you know, back in the States, they play baseball because it's, you know, it's what you grow up doing—there's just leagues and it's very recreational. But to come here, people are really committed to the game, even with the different skill sets, because you have to seek it out, you have to come and find it. And I think people are intrigued by it. I know people are always asking me how the team is doing. Where are the stats online, you know. We've got our National Team, we'll call it. I think people are excited by it. Funding is a challenge, so if we could get some more funding, [then we could] really build it out to be on par with other European leagues, which is the goal.

DJ. Is the team that's going down to the London tournament kind of the Scottish National Team?

RYAN. Yeah, that's the Scottish National Team. We've done it a couple of times—that tournament's had various different names and various organizers, but it's always the same sort of group of teams plus or minus some other ones. We've done it for a couple of years, and it's always been a good weekend.

STEVE. It would be great to have a coach here, because right now, [as] I'm sure you've heard and seen, it's run by players, and then when you're running it, you're not getting the training time.

DJ. How do you get kids, or even adults, coming out? Why baseball and not another sport? What would you say to them?

RYAN. [For] kids like me growing up through the school system, it's football or rugby and that's it. You know, football or rugby way through. [But baseball,] I think it's just something different. I always remember in high school that we had one football team for the whole, like, that year—you've got ninety kids in that year. So even if it's half and half—forty-five boys that all want to play football—you can only put eleven players in the pitch, and you've only got an hour and a half.

STEVE. It's a different skill set. I mean, you don't have to be fit enough to run ragged for ninety minutes, and you don't have to be able to tackle somebody at full [speed]. And a lot of these guys, well, not a lot, but there are a couple of guys here are who are slightly older than the rest, and you can still, if you've got the skill set, you can keep playing for a longer time without worrying about breaking your body.

DJ. What's it like with the clubs here all playing together? Is it pretty collegial with each other? Everybody sort of have a good community of people?

STEVE. One hundred percent. I think that's what brings people down. Like I was saying before, if you're coming out to play baseball in Scotland, it's because you really love the game. People here, they love the game, so you have that common bond right off the bat. Yeah, it's just about keeping the league going. Everyone wants to have fun.

RYAN. Yeah, everybody wants to keep the league going and wants to keep the teams rolling forward. There's obviously the competitiveness and the rivalry during the games, but after that, like, you can sit and have a beer. The All-Star Game at the weekend is a good example. You take all the teams, mix everybody up and put them in, and everybody has a great weekend. There is definitely a lot of community within the whole of Scottish baseball.

The players divide into two squads for tonight's scrimmage. Since the pitching machine is already on the field, they'll use it instead of live pitching. Six outs per side before changing the fielding team. There is a range of skills on display tonight—both in the batter's box and in the field—as you would expect with this mix of A and AAA players. Some have only been playing a year, while others have been playing their entire lives.

The third baseman makes a very nice basket catch in foul territory. The shortstop manages a bad hop and just nips the runner at first. A stocky guy with a moustache and long hair hits a ball into the top of the tree in right field on the fly that goes for a ground-rule double. Sylvain valiantly pursues a ball in the outfield, his cap popping off as he runs. The quality of play may be better tonight than it was in Aberdeen, though the level of enjoyment seems to be consistent.

My thoughts are interrupted by a slender man dressed in a sleek all-black baseball uniform and an orange San Francisco Giants hat. Below the hat sit chunky black glasses that frame his earnest face. Mickey Walton looks to be in his mid-twenties, though I will soon learn that he is actually thirty-three. I had noticed him earlier as he worked on the mechanics of his swing with a ball on a tee. Swing after swing, rituals of movement seeking to become muscle memory. He tells me that he has been playing baseball for seven years. I'm curious about what attracts someone born in Scotland, and who grew up playing football, to the game of baseball.

I ask if he likes the individual part of baseball, and he replies, "I like technicality and teamwork. The perfect combination because there's stats for yourself so that you can know what to work on, but also there's a team camaraderie. Whereas golf is slightly different, where you're just focusing solely on yourself, like a tennis player. But this is a bit more team-oriented." His answer leads me to ask if this is a good team, a good group of people to be around. Mickey doesn't hesitate to tell me that it absolutely is, both on and off the field. He goes on to say,

> Everyone's got that right frame of mind and motivation to enjoy the game and also to develop. Aska, over there, she'd never picked up the bat before a few years ago. She used to run. You

> know, just for fitness. Never been exposed to baseball before. She just turned up. She enjoyed the company of other people. People seem to be, you know—if you're struggling with something, there's always going to be other people wanting to help you and assist you. That's the mentality of this place. What's very attractive about this club is the people. The people make the club.

I notice that Aska has just come in from left field and approach her for a quick chat before she bats. She is in her late twenties and wears what looks like a tennis dress. Long hair flows from the back of the visor she wears instead of a ball cap. She's more reticent to talk than the rest of the team, but eventually she tells me that she has been playing for two years and that she approached the team herself. She had searched for baseball in Edinburgh online after she had seen baseball with her family in Japan. She goes on to tell me that she likes the community here because it's mainly younger people—people her age. I ask her, as I do with most people, about her favourite baseball memory: "It's not really one memory, but I think just being down here when it's ten p.m. and it's still sunny and we've just overran training and there's a few of us and it's just fun. That's one of my favourite things."

Training over, the team begins to pack up the equipment and take it back to the clubhouse. It's golden hour as I sit and finish the beer I was handed when the scrimmage began. As the players work, I look around the park and its idyllic setting and find myself hoping that these clubs will be able to have a permanent diamond here. I think about how much this organization and its teams mean to the people who are here tonight. Baseball is social and acts as a community for people, whether they come from somewhere else, like Caitlin and Sylvain and Steve and Aska, or were born and raised in Edinburgh, like Ryan and Mickey. They all just want to play, to keep playing, to pull together so that the team and the sport can survive in Edinburgh and in Scotland.

SUNDAY, JULY 9, 2023

Sunday morning in Stockbridge, just north of Edinburgh centre. The sun is shining on couples and young families as they stroll down Raeburn Place. Adults sip on coffee, wave greetings to each other, while children bop up and down in their strollers or toddle along beside their parents. There are lines at several of the bakeries, and I can smell the freshly baked pastries as I walk past. It's nice to be staying away from the crowds of tourists who throng Old Town and to be in a real neighbourhood, especially one as leafy and serene as this one.

Last night we had dinner with Deni Kasa, one of my former students. It's been seven or eight years since I last saw him, and it was good to catch up. He's been in Edinburgh less than a year, up from London for a new job in finance. It's a steep learning curve, and he has little time outside of work and studying for accreditation exams, but still, I want to know how he likes it here. He tells me it's beautiful—the gothic buildings and the castle on the hill—but that when the winter comes, the beauty seems to fade and it's just imposing, keeping everyone at arm's length. And the city as a whole feels like that, hard to penetrate, hard to get to know people. He's glad for the people at work, he says, or it would feel very lonely. I think of Caitlin and Steve and Aska and how baseball makes the city feel smaller. I hope that in amongst all the work and studying that Deni is able to find something similar.

I turn left off Raeburn Place on to Arboretum Avenue and then right onto the shaded path that follows the Water of Leith, past morning dog walkers and runners who come towards me at varying speeds. Up across Howard Street to Warriston Crescent and I'm back at Warriston Playing Fields, an hour early for the eleven a.m. game between the Diamond Devils and the Granite City Oilers. I'm here in time to watch them set up, transforming the empty space of the park into a functioning diamond for today's game.

Most of the Diamond Devils are already here, some carting things from the clubhouse across the park, others beginning to set up. The orientation of the diamond is in the opposite direction than it was on Friday night, so that the playing field now radiates northwest toward the clubhouse and storage area, from home plate that sits much closer to the park entrance. Sylvain squats behind home, determining the angle of the first and third baselines so that they can be measured and marked. A measuring tape runs from the point in the middle of the plate straight to the wooden "mound" that the Edinburgh teams use for home games. Constructed of wood and covered in astroturf, it consists of a flat platform about a foot and a half wide and ten inches high that slopes at perhaps a twenty-degree angle towards the batter. It looks like an injury waiting to happen.

Behind the plate, other players begin to assemble the temporary backstop: three panels of netting, perhaps ten feet at its highest point, that sit on metal runners and are anchored on each side with guy wires. As the players work, "Back in Black" blares from a boom box that sits next to the bats and gloves that await the game. Bases will be placed once the lines have been drawn. Out-of-bounds lines will be marked to each side of the baselines. Temporary orange fencing will ring the outfield. Set up takes almost as much time as the game itself.

As Sylvain intimated to me, the Edinburgh club would very much like to become custodians of the playing fields so they can put in a permanent diamond in the same orientation that they have arranged today. Right now, from what I've been told, the fields are really only used for school football and physical education; if not for the baseball teams, the fields would be extremely underutilized. At least that's the opinion of the team and its supporters. The key, of course, is to convince the City of Edinburgh Council that is the case and that the best solution is to put the fields under the stewardship of the baseball club.

As the work continues, Oilers players begin to arrive. Casey and Erin. Jackson. Laurence "Cammi" Cameron, one of the only remaining Oilers players from before COVID. Subin Gurung, who is originally from Nepal and who came to the Oilers from the Aberdeen University team. Matt McLean, a fellow Canadian. "Keep 'Em Separated" now plays on the boom box.

Field assembled, the Devils commence with batting practice as the Oilers offload their bags at their bench and begin to stretch. The familiar opening of "Lithium" drifts across park. I say hello to the Oilers I met last week and introduce myself to Matt. He's tall and lean, his face open and younger looking than I expect he is. Dressed in a blue Oilers T-shirt and white baseball pants, Matt is from Nova Scotia and moved to Aberdeen in 2020, just as the pandemic was beginning. He is, without doubt, the most experienced player on the Oilers, having played baseball since he was four years old. He continued playing into university, including club baseball at St. Francis Xavier University in

Antigonish, Nova Scotia. That was the end of his baseball career until he moved to Aberdeen and discovered the Oilers, a turn of events that he welcomed, both as a way to get back into the game and to meet people in the city. But there has been a lot of turnover, even in the two years that he's been with the team. I ask him about that lack of continuity, and he replies, "I think [it's] quite nice to have the kind of range of experience so you can kind of continue to grow the game with new people as well." No doubt true, but also diplomatic. Some might even say Canadian.

A man in his seventies, with long mutton chops and wisps of grey hair peeking out of his old blue ball cap walks the perimeter of the field, greeting people as he goes. Everyone seems to know him, so this must be Gordon "Wolfie" Dean. Almost all the players I spoke with on Friday night mentioned him, said he has stories upon stories about baseball in Scotland and that once you get him going, it's hard to stop him. This last bit was always accompanied by a wry smile, a hint that I couldn't know what they meant until I spoke with him myself. As Blur's "Song 2" starts up across the diamond, I step into the breach.

I walk over to where he stands, but he steps forward before I can say anything, me being probably the only person here he doesn't know. He extends his hand and says, "Kellogg's Corn Flakes. Battle Creek, Michigan." While I try to puzzle out what this might mean, I tell him my name and what I'm doing here and ask if I might talk to him for a few minutes. He nods and begins to tell me his story and the story of baseball in Scotland, emphasizing the ways in which they are intertwined and how so much of it comes back to his wife who passed away a few years ago. More than once his voice falters, as when he tells me, "I'll not leave my wife's grave. She died thirteen years ago, and I visit her grave twice a day." It's clear to me after only a few minutes that the loves of Wolfie's life are his wife and baseball, and that the two of them are inextricably connected.

His narrative weaves in and out and back on itself—sometimes sticking to baseball, but at other times drifting into American football and softball—so that it's at times quite hard to follow and harder still to piece together chronologically. But here's my attempt at getting down the bones of Wolfie's story. His mother was born in Scotland, across the Tay from Dundee, and his father was American. They lived in the US when he was a kid, which was where he learned to play baseball and where he fell in love with the sport. They moved to Scotland when he was thirteen. He moved to Aberdeen in 1976 and played on a team there against sides from US bases. Both at that time and while he was involved in later leagues, Wolfie's wife helped with organization and feeding the players. In 1988 he helped start the first Scottish league, which was in existence for ten years. He has played, umpired, and organized; he still umpires, as he will today. More than once during our talk, he says, "I've done it all." His life in baseball seems to swirl around us, enveloping me in stories and memory. If not for the start of the game, I think we might still be there.

There are seven people watching as the Devils, clad in jet-black jerseys emblazoned with *DIAMOND DEVILS* in red block lettering, take the field to the sound of Green Day's "When I Come Around." The start of the game is delayed as they try to find the game balls. From his position near first base, Wolfie yells, "I'm getting older by the minute." Finally, someone unearths the stash of game balls and tosses one to Sylvain, who will toe the makeshift mound for the Devils today. He told me Friday night that when he played in Australia, he threw in the low 80s and then went on to say, "I like pitching, but I'm past my years of pitching." He's back to pitching this season, though, for the first time in many years. His cutter doesn't work anymore, but he still has a bit of a slider. He doesn't throw as hard, but he can throw upwards of 150 pitches in an outing. At this level, you just need someone who can get the ball across the plate. At this level, Sylvain is still a more than viable pitcher. That's why he's out there, taking his life into his hands on the contraption that sits at the middle of the diamond. That first step off is a killer.

Jackson is first up for the Oilers, but he watches a called third strike from Sylvain. Cammi then hits the ball to the first baseman, who steps on the base as Wolfie gestures with his hand and yells, "O-U-T! Out!" Matt singles, then proceeds to steal both second and third. But that's as far as he gets, with the Oilers stranding two in the first.

Matt takes the mound for the bottom of the inning. It's not his natural position, but as I've seen and will see throughout the summer, anyone with previous baseball experience will be pressed to pitch at least some of the time. It's the reality of having so little pitching—in Sylvain's words, "None of the teams have pitchers." Today is Matt's turn, and the Devils quickly greet him with four runs to take the lead.

As I watch the game from behind the temporary backstop, one of the spectators comes over to talk. He's an older man, perhaps in his early sixties, dressed in a heavy jacket to ward off the chill that pervades the air despite the day's sunshine. His brown hair is straight, combed to one side, his face weathered from sun and wind. His name is Peter Bremner, and he tells me that he passed by one day about four years ago and sat down to watch. He didn't understand the game, so he asked questions, and then, week by week, the rules started to make sense. He liked what he was seeing: "I like the cosmopolitan feel about the place, so I just kept coming back." Most weekends he's here to watch, popping over from his flat a few blocks away. Sometimes he even comes out to watch training. The players all know him, and it all makes him feel like he's part of something.

"Hey, that's my mom!"

I turn from the game and from Peter to the Oilers' bench, where Erin is in mock outrage about Casey almost getting hit by a pitch. Casey is uninjured, gets back in the box, and draws a walk. She steals second and then scores from there on a groundout. Erin herself walks, but is thrown out trying to steal second. On the drive home, I'm sure that Casey won't let her forget how many steals each of them had. 4–1 Devils after an inning and a half.

In the bottom half of the inning, the Devils score seven off a combination of hits and errors. Despite the score, the two teams continue to compliment each other on good fielding plays and good hits. Partway through the inning, the boom box comes to life as Mickey cues up walkup songs for his teammates. The first is for Devon Greenshields, he of the moustache and long hair. As he walks to the plate, Marvin Gaye sings "Let's Get It On." From there we get "I Believe in Miracles (You Sexy Thing)," "I've Got the Power," and "Enter Sandman."

When the Oilers take the field for the bottom of the third inning, it's Kaoru Miyashita who climbs the temporary mound while Cammi takes over behind the plate for Jackson. Matt moves to his more natural position at shortstop and has barely settled in when the first batter hits a sharp ground ball deep in the hole to his left. Matt shuffles his feet, squares to the ball, and throws a laser to first. Wolfie's hand goes up as he says, "Who threw that?! I like it! He's out!" The next two batters proceed to hit balls between second and third, and each time Matt is perfectly positioned, ready to scoop and fire. 6–3 for all three outs of the inning. Matt has clearly played some ball—he's smooth and sound in his fundamentals at short. In this league, that alone would mark him as one of the better players. But when, in the bottom of the fourth, he ranges to his right, fielding the ball backhanded on one hop before planting and throwing to first, it's clear how good he really is.

I spend much of the game standing next to Ewan Spence, who is keeping score today and who, I soon discover, keeps score for most games played in Edinburgh. He's stockily built—what my mother would have called stout—with a round face that is framed by glasses and a salt-and-pepper beard. A big presence, Ewan laughs often, his dry wit ever present in his constant patter, and his enthusiasm is infectious. When we were first introduced before the game began, the first thing he said to me was "you've chosen to come to see two teams at the bottom of the league. How Scottish."

Ewan tells me: "Just before COVID, I heard the crack of the bat and went, 'Oh, I know that. What's that doing here?' That sound is not meant to be heard in Edinburgh." He followed his ear and walked down to where they were playing. He knew he didn't want to play, but since he was already a fan of the game through his love of the San Francisco Giants, he asked what they needed and how he could help. They asked him if he could keep score, and since he knew the basic rules and had spent the past ten years or so watching the Giants, he agreed. It was a decision that quickly led to his larger role as chief scorekeeper for the Edinburgh club, as he moved from being what he calls "a long-distance fan" to someone enmeshed in the game at a very different level. Keeping score live is, for him, a thrill and a challenge, but also a way to become more deeply connected to the game of baseball. He tells me, "In the same way they're learning what to do playing baseball, I'm watching and learning what needs to be done in terms of keeping score." He'll see something new in a game—and, let's face it, you always see something new in baseball—and realize that he needs to take another look at the rules so that the nuances don't escape him. As I watch, I see how meticulous he is, always wanting to make sure that he's getting the details right, honing what he sees as his chosen craft. It's his way of interacting with the game.

As we watch the teams change sides at the end of the fourth inning, Wolfie yells over to Ewan, "You're in my hall of fame. You know that!" Ewan smiles and says, "The team knows me. It's like it's a completely different social circle to the other ones—this is a complete switch off to other areas I have in life, but it's also a complete switch on to something else." Scorekeeping has given him a different relationship with baseball than he had during the years when the Giants were on in the background of his home office as he worked late into the night. For him, it's "very much a different way of playing." And it's not only the challenge of continually learning and trying to improve as he keeps score that has been and continues to be important, but also the move from being a solitary fan to being part of a larger, local baseball community.

It's 12–1 as we head to the top of the fifth. Subin leads off with a swinging bunt that he's able to beat out. They put another on, and Ewan turns to me and says, "Get yourself on base. That's one of the most important things in Scottish baseball." That is, of course, true in all baseball, but perhaps, I think, even more true at this level when almost anything can happen when the ball is put in play. Still, I want to make sure I understand what he's getting at, so I ask him to elaborate. He says, "Scottish baseball has a different flavour and feel. This is still very much—to use the vernacular—a small-ball league. And it's a league where it's probably easier to induce mistakes and errors than it is to induce great ball." As I watch the Oilers score six runs through a combination of walks, errors, and a couple of timely hits, I see what he means. Given my experience in Ireland, though, it seems to me that this observation applies to all leagues who play at this level.

The bottom of the fifth opens with another triple from Devon. As he rounds first base, Sylvain yells, "Be careful. You have bad knees!" Later in the inning, Jackson, who is no longer playing and is clearly bored on the Oilers' bench, wanders over to ask Sylvain about the bats they use. They are all custom-made, and Jackson wants to know where they get them. Sylvain explains that he and his father turn the bats themselves in France. I ask Sylvain if his father also played, but he laughs and says that his father just likes to work with wood and that making bats is just something they've always done. He goes on to tell me that the next time he goes to see his father, they will be doing ten bats for Tayport in their team colours.

By the time we get to the bottom of the sixth inning, the score is 16–8 for the Devils. Close to ending the game via the mercy rule, but not quite there. From the pitcher's mound, Sylvain yells what I think must be instructions to Devon at second base. Someone on the bench says, laughing, "That's French for 'don't be a dick.'" Ewan turns to me and says, "It's fun. We're out in the sun. Things are happening." He's right. Despite the score—the game will be called on a mercy rule later in the inning with the score 23–8—everyone still seems to be enjoying themselves playing baseball in the Edinburgh sun.

TAYPORT

Real baseball is about family. It's not about winning; it's not about trophies or any of that shit because at the end of the day we're playing in a grassroots league in the middle of nowhere and nobody knows we're here but us.

—JASON WEST, TAYPORT BREAKERS

THURSDAY, JULY 13, 2023

Back north on the train yesterday, over the Firth of Forth at Queensferry, up the coast to Kirkcaldy, and then straight north to Dundee. Clouds rolled across the blue of the Scottish sky. Fields of canola spread themselves from the tracks across to the distant hills. As we crossed the bridge over the River Tay, I gazed out the window to the right, tried to see where Tayport, home of the Breakers, might be. My plan had been to make my way over later today, but the dark clouds that now hung over the sea did not bode well for tonight's scheduled training session. Sure enough, after we had settled ourselves in our new flat, I got a WhatsApp message from Jason West, the Breakers' manager, saying that it had been called due to the weather. *But*, he wrote, *I can pick you up in the morning and we can talk then.*

That afternoon Heidi and I walked for a couple of hours to orient ourselves to the city that would be our home for the next ten days. The buildings in city centre fascinate me: grey stone facades softened by rounded corners, Gothic churches, occasional art deco structures, the stunning V&A Dundee that looms over the Firth of Tay like a ship that's bound for Norway. Boarded up windows that dot the city centre attest to hard times, but it's a city that already feels comfortable to me, compact, knowable. Later, we stopped for a beer at St. Andrews Brewing Company. Hearing my accent, the bartender, who introduced himself as Scott, asked where I was from and what I was doing in Dundee. I realized that, rather than assuming we were tourists as would have been the case in Edinburgh, he assumed we were here for some other reason, presumably work. I told him that I was writing about baseball in Scotland and so was spending some time with the Tayport team. Expecting him to say, "There's baseball in Scotland?" I was more than a little surprised when he said, "Oh yeah, my mate Liam plays for the Breakers." I made a note to track down Liam at the game on Sunday.

Jason's truck is already waiting on Trades Lane when I emerge from our building the next morning. After we introduce ourselves, Jason says, "Let me take you to my favourite spot for coffee." As he loops around and over the bridge, he starts to tell me about his background. His voice is deep and resonant as he talks, his Southern US accent always there, underneath but never pronounced, overlaid as it is by years of living in Scotland. Originally from Mississippi, he first came to Edinburgh in 2010 for an MA in English. There he met his future wife. He was back in the US for a couple of years but finally came to back Scotland to get married. They first settled in Glasgow for his wife's PhD, where Jason spent his nights playing country music in bars and his days working landscaping jobs. The move to this area happened when she took a job with the Gates Foundation; Jason was subsequently hired by the International College at the University of Dundee. When they moved, they needed a place that could accommodate their two dogs, and the decision to settle in Tayport had everything to do with wanting more space and fewer people around them.

As Jason talks, we cross over the Tay, the North Sea beckoning to our left, and then turn along the south shore of the river. Newport Road becomes Albert Street just beyond the green of the West Common and we're in Tayport. Soon Jason is turning left, pulling into a parking lot. I'm a bit puzzled as I don't see a coffee shop or restaurant or any kind of business. We get out of the truck, and I follow Jason to the rear of the vehicle. He pulls out a couple of camping chairs, hands one to me, grabs a thermos of coffee, and says, "It's just beyond those trees." As we move past the trees and across the wide expanse of the park, I see what he means. A baseball field next to the sea.

Dirt paths radiate from the angle crested with an arc that delineates the home plate area, and behind home plate is a permanent four-panel mesh backstop. In the middle of the clearly marked diamond is a permanent mound. Beyond the first baseline and the right field is beach grass and then the mouth of the Tay, the edge of the North Sea. Across the water, past right field, you can see Broughty Ferry in the distance. It is perhaps the most idyllic spot I've ever seen for a baseball field, and I can see why it is Jason's favourite spot for coffee. Sometimes, even when he's not working on the field, he just comes out here to sit and think.

Jason grins as we set up our chairs to the third-base side of home plate. He pours the coffee, leans back in his chair, cup in his large right hand, and surveys the field in front of him. He's a big man, a former football player, clad in shorts, Breakers hoodie, and ball cap. Sunglasses shade his eyes, and when he removes his cap, you can see that his hair is cut in a Mohawk. When he rolls his sleeves to his elbows, his heavily tattooed forearms are visible, ending in the hands of a lineman, fingers crooked from the beating they've taken through the years of down after down. His years of football are marked on his body, and the pain he carries with him is a constant.

He grew up playing football, his father a high school coach and athletic director who worked at a lot of different schools in Mississippi, taking many of them to championships. When Jason came to Edinburgh for his Masters, he was twenty-nine and hadn't played football for nine years, but when he found out there was an American football team at the university, he was drawn back in. After university, he played for Dundee for several years, making the drive up for games on the weekends. He then played for Glasgow when he moved there. Twenty-five years as a defensive tackle. "Thirteen too many," he says with an expression that's somewhere between a laugh and a grimace.

When he was in Glasgow, Jason started playing baseball with the Galaxy in addition to his time playing football. When he moved to the Dundee area, he first considered going back to coaching football, something he had done in his twenties in the US, but he found himself drawn to baseball instead: "I found that baseball was my way to get out of football. Even though I was never very good at baseball, I enjoyed it—I enjoyed the camaraderie around it. It gave me that same little piece of home that playing football here did." There was no baseball team in the area, but if he wanted to play baseball, he could have driven either south to Edinburgh or north to Aberdeen, as several others who lived here were doing. But one day when he was out walking the dog, he thought, Or we could just put a field right there. He points to the space in front of us as he tells the story about how the team started.

Thankfully, the Edinburgh Council saw value in adding something new to the park, and they were given permission to play here. At first, they brought in netting and threw down temporary bases, but they were soon given permission to create the more permanent diamond that is here now. They call it the Tom Waddell Memorial Baseball Field, named after the former major leaguer who was born here. Though he grew up in the US, his mother had been from Broughty Ferry and his father from Lochee.

At the end of 2019, they had some tryout days to judge interest. Forty people came to those initial sessions, and it looked like all systems were go. Then, in the spring of 2020, COVID hit, and it was well over a year until they had another game. A lot of people drifted away in the interim, but the people who were left were those who were most committed to the team and to baseball. They kept in touch over that summer, but because of the travel restrictions that were in place, it was only those on the Tayport side of the bridge who could even come to the field. With little else to do as he worked from home, Jason, with the help of Jake DeBurca, the only other player on the Tayport side of the river, set out to get the field in shape. It was something they could do outside, together but socially distanced. A project in the midst of days that often felt the same as the last. Carving it out of the site of this former landfill. Putting down screens to keep glass and other debris from unearthing. Backfilling with clean soil. Raking. Seeding. Pulling weeds. Making sure that the presence of the diamond was visually obvious, that baseball was carved into the landscape of this space by the sea.

But despite the visual iconography of the diamond seeming to claim a place in the park, they occupy the space in a way that is still tenuous, predicated as it is on a good working relationship with the Council. Their current deal is tenable for now as the Breakers only pay for the grass to be cut, with the players doing most of the grounds maintenance themselves. However, like the Edinburgh club, they are working on a long-term lease, an arrangement that would allow them to make additional improvements. The sticking point right now is not the Council but the cost of insurance for the permanent storage unit they would like to build, part of a larger investment in the infrastructure of the park. The ultimate long-term goal, though, is to acquire their own land somewhere along this stretch of coast and to develop a Scottish baseball complex modelled on Farnham Park in Slough.

When they were finally able to play in 2021, they proceeded to lose their first ten games. Half of the team had never played at that point, and there were mistakes galore. But by the end of the year, they were winning individual innings, as their players garnered more experience. Jason knew that he could organize, but he needed people who really knew the baseball side. It was with the addition of people like Hsinyen Lai, Marina DeAngelis, Paul Gardner, Ross Marnie, and David "Davey" Fair, that the team—half Scots and half expats—really began to take off. The next year, the Breakers won both the A and AAA championships, becoming successful much faster than even Jason could have imagined. He talks about the intensity of the games against the Glasgow Comets and the emotion that he felt and saw in all of the players when they finally won: "We all say it's just for shits and giggles, but it's something you don't get in your everyday life."

As pleased as he is with the team's success on the field, it's clear in talking to Jason that more important to him is the sustainability of baseball in Tayport and in Scotland. Several times he emphasizes that he always wants to put out the best nine he has and that they strive to win every game, but that their competitive drive is tempered by a desire to do so within the structure of the club, developing players and organizing the teams in such a way that baseball will be here in the long run. At one point he tells me, "I don't care about playing baseball that much. I didn't do this to play; I did this so that others would have a chance to play, and that kind of makes me feel good. The side of it I enjoy is seeing it grow, seeing it become something that wasn't there before." In the grassroots version of baseball, there are so many ways to carve out a relationship with the game.

As we talk, it becomes apparent that though he may not really care about playing the game, baseball has a deep place in his life, rooted as it is in his personal history and in the place he grew up. When he was a kid, people were at the ballpark every night in the summer. He tells me:

> In my mind, what baseball is is more akin to what I remember from Little League. It was a big part of my childhood even though I was never very good at it. So I'd like to see it exist to some kind of level like that here, and I think it absolutely could. And I think it needs to. There's nothing wrong with football, soccer, whatever, but you've got to give kids options because it's not going to be for everyone.

Having a child of his own has only solidified that commitment to youth baseball: "You want baseball to be a part of their lives if they want it to be one day. But you want it to be available and something sustainable for them, which is at the end of the day what we want to see." As was the case in so many other places I've been on this trip, his hope is to get into schools and to use the schools as a way to introduce the game and build the sport. It's incredibly difficult to make a sport sustainable without youth programs as a major component of growing the game, and it's nearly impossible to run youth programs without a large degree of volunteer support. There is no magic bullet, no easy way through, as Jason plainly realizes.

They could, he tells me, stop growing right now, both in terms of the development of the field and the overall program, and they could likely maintain what they have for ten or twenty years. As he so eloquently puts it, the Breakers and the league are both like potted plants that can be nurtured and sustained for a period of time, but that can only thrive when taken out of the pot and planted in the soil, nurtured in that local environment. For him and others around the country, it's about the long term and seeing this "develop into something that is Scottish, that is not just Americans in Scotland dicking around." This prompts me to ask him about what he thinks Scottish baseball is, and he replies, "I don't know yet. I don't think anybody knows yet, but I think there's a possibility for it." But he tells me it will have taken root when there is "a kid in the fourth grade seeing baseball played in his area and him not thinking, That's weird." Like so many others I've met in both Scotland and Ireland, Jason cares deeply about baseball and about seeing it become a part of the local fabric of sport. And that specific iteration of the game—whatever it looks like—is going to be Scottish baseball.

But Jason also understands that for baseball to take root, the onus and responsibility for the club has to branch out to include a larger community of people who are willing to do more than show up and play. He says, "It's starting to be that time for me to start passing it along—I'm not leaving, you know, but there are different things I could be doing. I need to be progressing and evolving as well. So somebody else needs to be the one stepping up and taking over some of the responsibilities. And they may take it in a different direction."

And while what happens at the club level is the most vital point of contact, without Baseball Scotland and the Scottish National Baseball League, teams would have no competitive outlet. As my conversation with Wolfie confirms, Scottish baseball has been around for several decades, but the league in its current form has not, formed only six years ago by "a handful of guys in the Perth train station having a couple of pints and writing stuff down on a notepad." There is intense competition between the teams, but at the core, they all realize—as is the case with the Irish Baseball League—that they need each other and that they need to work together. As Jason tells me, "What's clear is that there is passion for the game here. We don't always agree on what should be done or how it should be done, but there's no doubt there's a love for the game that exists here." The common goal of keeping the game going in Scotland is always the bottom line, and though he is mainly positive about the future, he's also realistic. I hear echoes of Sean Mitchell when Jason says, "The whole thing could roll up tomorrow. And really all it takes is a little bit of bad blood. It's a fragile, fragile thing."

I glance at my watch and realize that we've been talking for nearly four hours and could likely continue to talk for several more. As we finally begin to pack up, Jason turns to me, delivers a final thought: "Baseball is gonna be baseball. But it's developing that community and that feeling of family around it."

Our talk today adds to the palimpsest of the trip, becomes part of the larger conversation in my head about grassroots baseball in places where people don't expect to find it. What happens when there is no infrastructure, when there's just an idea and people pursuing it? When you begin with baseball stripped down to the studs? A game that develops organically through the hard work and cooperation of many people. This is Scottish baseball. This is Irish baseball.

SUNDAY, JULY 16, 2023

It's just after nine a.m. when I emerge from our flat and walk to the bus station at the end of the block. While waiting, I notice a peeling mural of Dennis the Menace on a brick wall in an area that is fenced off, across the forecourt from the depot building. Dundee is the home of D.C. Thomson, publisher of *The Beano* and *The Dandy*, which feature characters such as Desperate Dan, Minnie the Minx, Oor Wullie, Dennis the Menace, and Gnasher. Officially sanctioned bronze statues of these characters dot the landscape of the city centre, but this is the first piece of graffiti I've seen, and it fittingly depicts Dennis aiming his slingshot at the viewer. As I try to get a good photo of it and the other graffiti, a woman from the transit company rushes over, yelling at me to get away from this area where passengers are not allowed. I manage to get the shot before retreating to the safety of the depot to await the bus to Tayport for today's game.

The bus loops around to the bridge along the same route I had taken with Jason a couple of days ago. As we cross the river, I look back at the Dundee waterfront, from the condos just to the south of our flat, east to the cranes and towers of Dundee Port, and beyond to Broughty Ferry. Ahead I see the patchwork of green to our left where the road bends south at Tayport, where I plan to get off so I can walk the town before I'm due at the field for today's game.

I let the stop at Victoria Road pass and alight from the bus at Tayport Parish Church, aiming to walk along Castle

Street to the mouth of Tayport Harbour and then back along Tay Street to School Wynd and eventually the Promenade. From there I will be able to walk along the shore until I reach the ballpark. It's a sleepy Sunday morning, and the streets are empty as I pass the post office, a pharmacy, and a tattoo parlor, all shuttered at this early hour. Across the road, on the main floor of a converted house, tall chimneys flanking either end of the two-storey brick structure, is Tayport Premier. It's a small store, its windows covered in advertising, some indicating that they have food and coffee on offer. My stomach rumbles, reminding me that I've had nothing but coffee this morning. I think about crossing the road, giving my custom to the store with the large *Welcome to Tayport* sign, but the Co-op is right in front of me and it is also open. I duck in, grab a sausage roll, and continue down the hill to the harbour. At the water, I watch the sailboats moored on the inner side of the breakwater as I sip my coffee and eat my roll. I walk past the Bell Rock Tavern and stare across to Broughty Ferry and the castle we visited yesterday. It's a sunny day, but the wind makes it cool by the water.

Back along Tay Street, I look at the houses that line the road and wonder about the people within, who are at their breakfast or getting ready for church or the golf course or simply sleeping in on a Sunday morning. I wonder how many of them know that there will soon be baseball just down the road, on a beautiful field by the water. I wonder how many even know there is baseball in Tayport or even in Scotland. I wonder how many would care.

As I approach the water, I see the tidal flats stretching east, pockmarked zones of green and brown and blue that extend far into the Firth and the sea beyond. A long stick rises out of the flats to my left, the only perpendicular marker in a flat plane that shimmers brown and blue as the sun reflects off its surface. In the distance, a woman and her dog walk along the glistening sand and rocks, the dog sometimes chasing a stick and sometimes just walking beside her. Nearing them, I see that it's a big black lab and that he seems to match his owner's big black puffy coat. The dog runs after one of the many shore birds who peck for food. The woman calls him back, gives him an affectionate pat, and sets off again in the direction of the harbour. Sunday morning by the sea.

Rounding the corner from the caravan park, I see two figures on the mound at the far end of the open green space. Others are laying down the bases and raking the area around home plate. Players from the Breakers getting ready for what will be an intrasquad game. When I was planning this trip, the Oilers were scheduled to be down for a AAA game and the Edinburgh Knights were scheduled to be up for an A game, but it became apparent in the past week that both clubs would be unable to field a travel team. Then the Edinburgh Rays, scheduled to come to Tayport next week, indicated that they could come a week earlier, but through some kind of miscommunication that also fell apart. As Jason would tell me later, he knew I'd come a long way to see a game here, so he rallied as many players as he could from their overall membership so that they could mount an intrasquad game, an effort I appreciate immensely. Of course, forfeits are not out of the ordinary in leagues like this one when significant travel is involved, especially for teams that play at the edge of the league's catchment area. The Renegades similarly announced yesterday that the Ashbourne Giants would not be making their way to Cork today so they too would be playing an intrasquad game. Such is the reality of grassroots leagues, and as Jason texted me, *Such is the life of a UK manager*.

There are already about fifteen spectators here—friends and family, I assume—as the players continue to work on the field, the sound of trimmers and blowers layered over conversations and the increasing roar of the wind. I put down my bag near where we sat a few days ago and shake hands with Jason, who has just finished setting up a pair of enormous tower speakers in front of the team van. A black Mitsubishi Delica from the late 90s, the van is part rolling equipment storage and part road-trip facilitator. It sports a bank of lights on its roof and an extended grill that would act as an excellent battering ram if they ever needed to make a quick getaway. There are dings all over the body—presumably from foul balls—and its proximity to the field all but ensures that there will be more before the end of the day. Extra bases cover the windshield to prevent a shower of glass and a bill the club—and Jason—does not need. Yesterday he told me a story about a buddy of his from back home who just bought a bass boat. I wondered where this was going before he added, "I don't go to the pub. I don't fish any more. This is my bass boat." The Breakers is where his time and energy and, to some extent, money go. If the windshield cracks, it will be on him, at least initially, to get it fixed.

Finished with the sound system, Jason turns on a game-day mix, and the first notes of "Take Me Out to the Ballgame" float across the park, adding to the palimpsest of sound. He then points to a lightly bearded man in his late thirties just taking off a Mets warmup jacket and says, "That's Liam Quinn." I introduce myself, tell him about meeting Scott at the brewery. Liam smiles broadly, his eyes crinkling into well-worn laugh lines. Originally from Portrush in Northern Ireland, Liam tells me that he didn't know there was any baseball in Ireland when he lived there.

It was seeing Ken Burns's *Baseball* just before lockdown that initially piqued his interest, the history acting as a gateway to exploring the current game. A couple of friends followed MLB teams, and as he began to watch, he eventually took up with the Mets. At first, his interest was focused solely on watching the game, and when he first googled Baseball Scotland, he was simply looking for people with whom he could watch and talk about the game. But after a move from Manchester to Dundee, he found not only other people interested in baseball, but also, in the Breakers, a chance to learn to play the game, a sport that could replace the football he felt he could no longer play.

As we talk, Liam becomes more and more animated, and tells me, "I never thought I'd get obsessed with a sport again. That's what you do when you're younger." He goes on to talk about the excitement he experienced in following Celtic in his youth before saying he feels that way again now about baseball: "I've got that passion back, which is lovely, to integrate that into my life at a later stage." He laughs often as he talks about learning the intricacies of the game and how much he enjoys thinking about what's really going on even when it seems like not much is happening on the field, both when he watches and when he plays. Like so many of us, he's attracted to the fact that in baseball there's always something more to learn, whether you're playing, watching, or keeping score. But, as a player, he also appreciates how everyone on the field participates, an aspect of baseball that is fundamental to the game and so different from a sport like football. As Liam puts it, "I just love the fact that everyone—it doesn't matter how good a team you're playing—it's so fair. Everyone gets a chance to hit. You really do get a fair crack at the whip, and that's just beautiful, I think." He's only in his second year, but it's a game that he sees himself continuing to play, despite being too busy at work to come out much this year. In fact, he is here today only because Jason called and urged him to come.

We finish our chat, and Liam makes his way out to the field for some pre-game warmup. I'm watching the players begin to take their places for infield practice when I notice a middle-aged couple and an older man sitting, watching the action from lawn chairs set back on the third-base side of the diamond. Thinking they must be family or friends of one of the players, I introduce myself, interested in hearing their perspective on the game and on baseball in Tayport. Their names are Jen and Leighton Pritchard, and as we talk, I discover that they don't have any connection to a specific player as I assumed—and as had been assumed about me so many times during the summer of watching games for *100 Miles of Baseball*—but are here simply because they like baseball. They first encountered the sport on a trip to Boston where they saw a game at Fenway Park. On subsequent trips to the US, they have tried to see a game wherever they are. When they heard there was live baseball in Tayport, they started to come out, partially because of their own interest and partially as an outdoor activity they could do with Leighton's father, who tells me he likes it and that it reminds him of the cricket he watched when he was younger. As we talk, my attention is drawn to the two players—a young man and young woman—taking turns fielding ground balls in the left side of the infield. They're both fluid in their movements as they judge the hop of the ball, set themselves, scoop, and fire crisply and accurately across the diamond to first. But as I watch them take their reps, it starts to become clear that it's second nature for the woman; her footwork, glide to the ball, and transition from glove to throwing hand are all muscle memory, clear evidence that she's been playing this game for a long time. The young man is good, but you can tell that there is still a thought process that precedes the mechanics of fielding, that it hasn't yet moved from conscious thought and into the muscle as it has for the young woman.

I walk over to Jason at the van, ask him who we're watching in the field. "That's Marina DeAngelis, from Canada. Great player and has been really important as a coach for us. And he's Shane Sures. One of those guys with the right attitude. Does whatever needs to be done. You should talk to both of them, and be sure to also speak with Hsinyen."

I see Marina walking over to speak with a couple of people who are out for the first time today, and so I approach Shane. His grey pinstriped jersey vest, with *Tayport* in blue cursive script across the chest, covers a blue compression shirt. The Breakers' logo—an ornately intertwined *T* and *B*—appears on both his blue cap and his grey pants. He tells me that he is also from Canada—Markham, Ontario—and that he's moving back there in the next couple of weeks. In fact, today will be his last or perhaps second last game with the Breakers. He moved to Scotland in 2019 to study physiotherapy at Robert Gordon University in Aberdeen—in the same program as Marina—and then moved to Dundee to work in 2021. Given what I've seen during infield practice and the rifle he has for an arm, I'm surprised to hear him say that he never played baseball as a kid. He says, "I already knew the game. And it's welcoming here—the level's not crazy high because everyone is new. It's just so friendly, so fun. You get all skill levels, but no one really cares." In that mix of skill levels and with the support of his teammates, Shane has progressed rapidly as a ballplayer, taking to the game as if he were simply picking it back up after some time away. Since it is perhaps his last game, he's going to ask Jason to let him play a different position every inning.

I leave Shane to his quest and make my way over to Marina. Like Shane, she's in her late twenties, but she wears a blue pinstriped jersey vest over a blue compression shirt with her Tayport hat and matching pants. Today she and Shane will be on opposing sides for the intrasquad game. She tells me that she's from Delta, British Columbia, and has been playing baseball since she was four years old. In grade ten, she started attending a high school with a baseball academy. She moved from there to Douglas College and then to Simon Fraser University, where she played both baseball and softball. Along the way, she played for a number of years with the BC Women's Provincial Team. After university, and before coming to Scotland, she played for a couple of years in an over-thirty men's league. Like other expats to whom I've spoken, Marina googled *baseball in Scotland* when she moved to Aberdeen, and while she attended Robert Gordon, she played for both the Oilers and the Express when the Aberdeen club had enough members for two squads. She says, "My first year there was the first year of the Express, so I was put on the Express team. And I remember meeting the guys at the pub the first or second night I came to Scotland—meeting the guys from the Oilers—and they're like, 'So you've played baseball before?' 'Yeah, I've played baseball before.' And they're like, 'Okay, you're a pitcher now.'" That season she became the first woman to start a game in the Scottish National League and was extremely successful in her transition to pitching; in one game at the end of August 2019, Marina notched fourteen strikeouts in seven innings against the Edinburgh Cannons as part of thirty-two Ks in nineteen innings pitched that season.

Though she has often played on men's teams, Marina tells me that she really valued her time playing with the BC Women's Open Provincial Baseball Team: "We all have that kind of shared experience of maybe being the only female playing on our team growing up through the years and kind of sticking with it. And then we finally get to come together as a group of females. 'This is so cool—we can all play together; we have the same kind of passion for it.'" As she talks, I hear the hints of a Scottish accent creeping in to her voice, especially in the way she punctuates her sentences with "erm," the pause a slight hitch in her mainly Canadian speech. I ask her about moving between baseball and softball, particularly in terms of hitting. She laughs and says, "I have my baseball coaches, and they would say, 'Marina, you have such a softball swing,' and then I have my softball coaches saying 'You have such a baseball swing.' And I'm like, 'No, it's just my crappy swing. It's the same for each sport. It's not good—I'm trying to change it." But, according to Jason, in this league she more than holds her own at the plate.

I ask about her transition to coaching since she's come to the Breakers. She tells me that she really enjoys it, but that it's sometimes hard to balance coaching and her own development as a player. But, finally, she has tried to move from thinking of self to thinking about the wider picture:

> What can I offer to the sport here? Once I've kind of taken on that role, taking a step back from my own ego, [I think,] Let's see if we can try to grow the sport here a little bit. And that's been really, really fun, and I really, really do like coaching people that are quite new to the sport. I feel that's probably where I have more to offer. I feel

> like coaching high level, I'm always really selfish because I want in there. I want to be taking reps. I want to be taking grounders.

Before she takes her leave to join the blue team, I ask her if she can sum up what it's like to play baseball in Scotland. She mentions the commitment that's needed to come and help set things up, the way you have to play through frequently inclement weather. Then she pauses and says, "You've got to really love the sport to play here."

Shane will start today for the Grey team—Jason and his teammates have agreed to the plan, so this will be the first of seven positions he will play. Hsinyen Lai, the other coach and one of the main pitchers for the Breakers, will start for the Blue team. As the Grey team takes the field, I watch the dust swirl around the infield and listen to the roar of the wind off the water; I can barely keep my hat on and notebook open. It's going to be an adventure today for the outfielders.

In Shane's stint on the mound, he walks Marina and hits Liam, giving up a couple of runs along the way. In the bottom of the inning, Marina makes two very nice plays at shortstop, ranging first to her left before firing a strike to first base and then playing an in-between hop perfectly to get the final out of the inning. Shane dons the catching gear for the top of the second and gets behind the dish to warm up Ryan Mandala, another of the Breakers' staff, and the new pitcher for the Greys.

As Ryan warms up, I wander over towards first base to get another angle on the game and to speak with Ross Marnie—unable to play today, but coaching first instead. When Jason pointed him out to me, he told me that his nickname on the field is "Bash." He sports a full sleeve of tattoos on each arm—red roses and green leaves encircle the right, while a ship and stylized waves feature on the left—and even under his light jacket, it's easy to see that he's well-built. His head is shaved, but his beard is full. There is, at first glance, an air of intimidation about him, but once you get him talking, his frequent smile dispels that impression.

Born and raised in Arbroath, a small town just north of Dundee, Ross started playing eight years ago with the Aberdeen club. "I always watched it. I watched it all the time," Ross says, "[but] I never thought I'd get to play." Like Shane, he picked it up quickly, playing not only for the Oilers and now the Breakers, but also for All-Scotland teams, like the one that will go to the British Baseball Federation Summer Cup in Slough next weekend. His path to the Breakers came at the confluence of wanting to play closer to Aberdeen after the birth of his first child and the call he received from Jason West about the possibility of getting a team together in Tayport. "Me, Jason, and Jamie [Keith] sat in a bar one night. 'All right, how are we gonna get this team going?' The three of us are gonna do it. That was it." Jamie only played for one season, moving away from baseball to focus on coaching football, but Ross and Jason have stayed the course, despite their one-win inaugural season. I ask about community on this team. Ross replies, "To be honest, the community in baseball in Scotland is pretty good. When you're playing Aberdeen or Glasgow away, everybody's just good friends. It's a good day out. It's a really good community, I think, because we're not huge. We don't have as much money as soccer and rugby and things like that, so everybody kind of does what they can to prop the game up."

As we talk, Grey scores three runs, making the score 4–3 Blue as we move to the top of the third inning. Ross and I walk back to where Jason stands near the van. Shane has moved to first base for this inning, while Ryan Mandala is on to pitch for a second inning. A grounder is scorched down the line, and the third baseman makes a nice pick before firing across the diamond. Jason tells me that's Paul Gardner—"PG," as everyone calls him—one of the stalwarts of the Breakers and of baseball in Scotland. He may be one of the older players, but he's smooth on the field, hustling on every ball hit to third. In the top of the fourth, he will make another nice scoop; in the sixth, he'll have two 5–3 putouts, including a play in which he will have to charge the ball on a slow dribbler past the mound. But that's all to come. Right now, it's still 4–3 Blue heading into the bottom of the third.

Shane leads off with a walk for Grey. He then proceeds to steal second and third, coming home on an overthrow to tie the score at 4–4. Jason points to a spot between third base and home and tells me that there they found what they thought was a very large rock when they were first constructing the field. As they began to unearth it, however, they soon discovered that it was actually a hearthstone that was so large that it had to be jackhammered out of the ground. When fully excavated, they saw it was carved with a masonic symbol, and as they researched, they discovered it was likely from around the 1890s. I ask where it is now, and Jason points to the other side of the van, beyond where they've sculpted the field. It's still there, hidden under the weeds.

While the Blue team bats in the top of the fifth with the score still tied at 4, I'm able to speak with Hsinyen. He tells me that he is originally from Taiwan and has been playing baseball since he was seven years old, just like every other kid around him. He played shortstop then, but when he moved to Scotland in 2012, he started pitching. He played with the Edinburgh Diamond Devils from 2012 to 2018, but he stopped playing when he finished his PhD in Politics at the University of Edinburgh and began to look for a position. In January of 2019, he joined the School of International Relations at the University of St. Andrews. When Jason discovered that Hsinyen was in the area, he reached out, and Hsinyen resumed his baseball career. I ask him if it took much convincing. He laughs and shakes his head, before going on to say:

> Baseball is a huge part of my life because baseball has taught me so many things, not just skills. I think its most important teaching is philosophy, a life compass, because it's a team sport, right, and for many games there's no one who can kind of dominate the game and decide whether this team is going to win. There are so many contingent factors that can affect the result. So I think that's how I learn from baseball.

Coming back to play was an easy decision, but Jason also asked if he would consider helping out with the coaching. I ask about his reaction to that request, and he tells me that he didn't have to think about it long either. "I think it's just part of my personality." He laughs as he says, "I like to share—I mean, teaching is just my job. I teach for a living." He goes on to tell me that it's easy working with a bunch of people who love baseball and are eager to learn, to improve as players and as a team.

Hsinyen reaches down for his glove and begins to walk to the mound for the bottom of the fifth. Shane is quickly aboard again, taking a big lead off second. Hsinyen makes a nice pickoff move, but Shane gets back just under Marina's swipe tag. On the next pitch, he steals third and again comes home on an overthrow. 5–4 Grey. The inning ends when Marina makes a very tricky catch behind second on a pop-up swirling in the wind. As the Blue team walks off the field, I look up past the van and see two horses—a pinto and a chestnut—trot across the tall grass in the space just to the left of the field. The presence of baseball seems to have little effect on them or their riders, focused as they are on their own day out. If you see something new every time you go to a baseball game, here it is for today's game, at least for me.

The score remains 5–4 Grey going into the top of the seventh, thanks in part to two nicely executed fielding plays by Marina from her spot on the mound. Blue score two in the top of the inning and Grey score one in the bottom half, the game ending fittingly in a 6–6 draw. In the bottom half of the inning, Davey Fair throws a bullet from his catcher's position to get Ryan stealing third, and the final out of the day comes when Liam makes a difficult running catch in centre field. When the game ends, Shane has managed to play every position except centre field and right field, and he has made some good plays as he moved around the diamond. There has been a lot of good defence today—from Marina, Shane, Paul, Ryan, Shane, Liam, Hsinyen, and Davey. It's easy to see why they've been successful in a league where limiting mistakes is crucial.

As the players begin to pack everything up for the day, I approach Ryan for a chat. He's been in Scotland for three years and has played for Tayport for the entirety of the club's existence. Growing up, he played on travel teams and continued throughout high school, but then stopped, taking the game back up only when he moved to Scotland in his mid-twenties. I ask him about starting to play again, and he replies,

> I was never really focused as a kid in terms of realizing that at practice [I should] actually [be] making improvements and getting better. And so I feel

> like I always had untapped potential just because I didn't have the mindset to go out every day and work for practice. I feel like this is sort of my second chance at that a little bit, just in terms of it's the first time I'm actually watching videos and working on my swing and focusing on my mechanics. It's given me a second chance at improving.

We talk a bit more about the team, about baseball in Scotland, about how to grow the game by getting kids involved. The equipment has been loaded in the van, and everyone seems ready to head for their vehicles. Before we leave, Jason says, "Here," and hands me a Tayport Breakers hat with its ornately intertwined *T* and *B*. I thank him, and he nods, shaking my hand again. Liam offers to give me a lift back to Dundee. It's been a good day out.

THURSDAY, JULY 20, 2023

Last night Heidi and I met Liam at the Wine Press in Dundee. We have a lot in common—baseball, of course, but also music, books, and film. When we finished our drinks, Liam told us he wanted to take us somewhere interesting for a nightcap, a "secret *shebeen*" we shouldn't miss before we left Dundee. He led us down Dock Street and along Whitehall until we got to a dark alley called Couttie's Wynd. Liam caught my look to Heidi and laughed. "I know, it feels more than a bit dodgy. We'll know the place is open if the light is on outside the unmarked door." We found the door and the light and proceeded down a set of narrow stairs lined with vintage advertising posters. A short hallway greeted us at the bottom, and once we passed through a dark curtain, we were suddenly in a joint that felt like it was transported from the southside of Chicago, circa 1925. Behind the narrow bar was exposed brick that framed rows of liquor bottles lit from beneath with a soft light. Simple stools with ornately wrought iron legs lined the polished wood bar, its top gleaming and its front ornamented with panels of pressed tin. High, narrow benches and tables were arrayed along the other walls. A long rectangular mirror seemed to float above one of the banks of benches. We settled in and ordered cocktails from the bartender, whose flat cap, moustache, and leather apron were perfectly suited to the atmosphere of the bar. He asked what we were doing in Dundee, and when I mentioned my project, he said that he played for a former Dundee team and briefly trained with the Breakers. It seems that the confluence of bartenders and Liam Quinn is the key to people knowing something about baseball in Scotland.

Tomorrow we leave for Slough on the 6:55 a.m. flight to Heathrow. It's hard to believe that my time in Scotland is up already. As I've travelled here and in Ireland, I've seen not only how much baseball means to people, but how many different things baseball offers to them. A community. Second chances. A way to rediscover the game. A way to focus. The chance to play a sport that has a place for everyone, not just the most fit. Baseball is competition, yes, but it's also family and camaraderie. It's a connection and shared stories. It's the individual within the collective. The quiet moments. The strategy. It's a game that takes a lifetime to master. It's seeing something new every game. It's the places that it's played. It's the people. It's the dedication of people to keeping the game going, niche sport that it is, because baseball here is always precarious, dependent on volunteers to do everything from scheduling games to maintaining the fields to coaching to keeping score. It's a shared passion for the game and a commitment to keep it moving forward, to not let it die. It's considered an American sport, but it's Irish baseball or Scottish baseball, a game that must grow where it is planted, subject to those specific contexts of place and time.

SLOUGH

You can place a baseball club anywhere, but
in order for it to grow, it's got to have the
right environment, the right stuff to feed it.

—PAUL CONVOY, BASEBALL SCOTLAND

SATURDAY, JULY 22, 2023

We arrived in Slough yesterday afternoon, the bus from Heathrow dropping us off just around the corner from our hotel. Heidi stopped just long enough to leave her larger suitcase before walking to catch the train for her weekend sojourn to visit Jane Austen's House in Chawton and Gilbert White's house in Selborne. My weekend would be taken up with the British Baseball Federation Summer Cup at Farnham Park, starting first thing on Saturday morning.

The only thing I knew about Slough when I arrived yesterday was that the British version of *The Office* was set here, so I decided to explore the town, or at least the city centre area near the hotel. I walked south a block to what appeared to be a main junction. Across the street was The Moon and Spoon, one of the ubiquitous Wetherspoon's pubs that can be found in every town in the UK. I turned left, down a street busy with pedestrians. As I walked, it soon became apparent that this was the high street, bustling with chatter and commerce. The buildings were a mix of late Victorian and more modern brick two-storey affairs, each with small shops and restaurants at street level. Shops that sold both mobile phones and vapes. Betting shops. Hardware stores. Takeaway shops. Sit-down restaurants. Produce shops. Grocery stores. The sign on Adam's Fruit proclaimed *Arabic, Asian, European Frozen Food & Grocery*, while two doors down Al Mubarak Halal Meat and Grocery's sign read *Asian, Somalian, Mediterranean Food*. The restaurant in between the two advertised *falooda*, *paan*, and Asian street food. Around me, I could hear at least a dozen different languages as people whose families had come from all over the world passed me by. Here, at least, was not the land of bleak corporate estates I had come to expect from *The Office*.

As I took the bus out to Farnham Park this morning, I began to see at least a bit of that landscape, the vibrancy of city centre replaced by the staid functionality of office parks. But turning north, the built environment yields to a brief oasis of green where I exit the bus and cross the road to the National Baseball & Softball Complex at Farnham Park.

Open since 2013, the park has two full-size fields that can be used for baseball or softball, with a diamond for each on opposing ends, as well as three smaller multi-purpose fields. It is, without doubt, the best baseball facility in the country, its two main diamonds as good as any you will see in amateur baseball in North America. All five fields will be in use this weekend to accommodate the twenty-four teams here to compete, eight in each of Gold, Silver, and Bronze Divisions that more or less correspond to the UK's AAA, AA, and A levels. In each division, there will be two groups of four teams, each of which will play the others in the group. The group winners will then play for the Gold, Silver, and Bronze championships. It's a lot of baseball for a two-day tournament, and consequently, there will be a two-hour time limit on all games, with no new innings after an hour and forty-five minutes.

At the end of the dirt road that leads into the complex is a squat building that houses the Home Plate Bar and Kitchen, the concession stand and pub for the park and the de facto headquarters for the tournament. I stop to double-check the schedule and grab a cup of coffee before walking across to my first game of the day—Baseball Ireland vs. the Croydon Pirates.

Jason Wiebe is sitting with a few other people from the Irish contingent on the stands behind home plate. Like me, he's wearing several layers, topped with a rain jacket to perhaps ward off the dark clouds that gather above us. He smiles, extends his hand, and tells me that he has something for me before opening his duffel bag and pulling out an Ashbourne Giants cap. It's just like the one he is wearing except that the outline of the block *A* is in purple rather than red. I thank him, and he smiles, then introduces me to Vanessa Collins and David Fowler, whose sons, Brandon Collins and Cian Fowler, are playing for the Irish team. In fact, it's mainly young players from the Academy, along with a few older players, including Pedro Juárez, Jimmy Pita, Alan Fox, and Trevor Peacock from the Dublin Spartans. It will be a good test for these young players to compete against the other teams in the Gold Division.

Some of the Irish players are playing catch beyond the third baseline, while others stretch in front of their dugout. They are all dressed in crisp white pants, green ball caps inscribed with white harps, and dark green jerseys with *IRELAND* in cursive across their chests. I see Sean Mitchell pacing in front of the dugout, green warmup pulled over his uniform against the chill of the wind. He's watching the Croydon infield practice intently. The team consists mainly of guys in their late twenties and early thirties who look comfortable fielding grounders, turning an imaginary double play. Above their white pants, they wear white jerseys that, in the bottom half and at the base of the short sleeves, feature horizontal stripes in various shades of brown. They wear black hats with gold brims that feature a stylized *P* in the same font as their jerseys, a riff, I think, on the Astros uniforms from the 1970s, even down to the rounded, block font used for the *CROYDON* that floats above the stripes. From South London, the Pirates regularly field AAA, AA, and youth teams; in this tournament, they will have teams in the Gold and Bronze Divisions.

I turn to Vanessa to ask her about Brandon and about her experience with baseball in Ireland. They had been living in Texas when her husband Chris took a four-year contract in Ireland. Brandon was sixteen at the time, had been playing travel baseball, and didn't want to give the sport up. So Chris searched out baseball in Ireland, ultimately getting in contact with Tom Kelly of the Dublin Hurricanes, the club which Brandon ultimately joined and with whom he continues to play. She tells me that, not only for Brandon, but for them as a family, baseball was a place to land that made them feel less like outsiders. Now, after two years of working with Frank Andrews every day at Strike Zone, Brandon will be playing baseball at a junior college in the US. As we talk, Vanessa opens her scorebook and begins to record the starting lineups. I ask her if that's something she regularly does, and she replies, "As a mom, I was like, 'I'm going to start keeping a scorebook because it keeps me out of trouble.' But it also gave me something to talk to Brandon about. You know, because as a mom, it's all about sports and Mom doesn't know anything about that." She laughs as she goes on to say, "So now we can talk about plays that he did and what happened. So that gave us a new, better relationship.

Until you point out a mistake he made." Now she's really laughing, a wide smile spread across her face at the thought of these conversations.

Vanessa hurries to finish preparing her scorecard as the managers and umpires meet at home plate, along with a fifth man, dressed in black as if ready to step in behind the plate at any time. The huddle breaks, and we are ready for the game to begin.

Ireland takes the field, Patrick Mitchell on the mound to start the game, with Cian—at only fifteen—behind the plate. Tall and lanky, Patrick's delivery is smooth, his right leg windmilling towards third as he releases the ball. A swinging strikeout to open the game, followed by a groundout to third base. A walked batter moves to second on a wild pitch but is stranded there by Patrick's second strikeout of the inning. Two more strikeouts in the second inning bracket a tough chance to Pedro Juárez at third and an exceptional scoop out of the dirt by Alan Fox at first to get the out. Patrick's fastball is crisp today, making his occasional change effective, and his slider completely fools right-handed hitters when it drops away and out of the strike zone. But despite managing a couple of baserunners, Ireland cannot score either, and the score remains 0–0 going into the top of the third inning.

Two singles, an error, and a double later, it's 3–0 for Croydon and Patrick's day is done. Brandon Collins comes on to replace him, inducing a fly ball to centre and a groundout to third to end the inning. Ireland loads the bases in the bottom of the inning on a ten-pitch walk from Pedro, but they aren't able to cash in as a flyout to right field ends the inning. Walks and errors haunt Ireland in the bottom of the inning as Croydon scores five runs without a hit, making the score 8–0.

With the game beginning to get out of hand, my attention begins to wander to the Liverpool Trojans, who have congregated on the berm behind the diamond. Jason waves at one of the players, who then comes over to where we are sitting. Jason introduces him as Michael Walsh, an American based in California who has played in Ireland and with Irish teams. When Michael hears about what I'm doing this summer, he becomes animated and begins to tell me about his connection with baseball in Ireland and the UK. He travelled to Ireland in 2013 for The Gathering—an effort to entice the Irish diaspora to return—and played there in a baseball tournament at Corkagh. Since then, he's been travelling to Europe to play baseball: "I'd go home to work, but then during the summer I'd come back. I play baseball in California in a men's league. I travel to Arizona during the week—I have a baseball problem." He laughs and goes on to tell me that he met Ian Blease, the manager of the Trojans, at the World Baseball Classic in Arizona and told him that he would love to play in and for Liverpool in the summer. And now here he is. Before he makes his way back to his current teammates, he says, "I want to just play on every continent. That's the goal."

As Ireland bats in the bottom of the fourth, once again leaving the bases loaded without scoring, I approach the man who was in the pre-game meeting at home plate with the umpires and managers. His name is Gabor Erdos, and he is in charge of the umpires for the tournament this weekend. He's been an umpire now for thirty years, umpiring and also playing in his native Hungary, a country that initially had much less uptake of baseball than did many other countries in Eastern Europe. When he moved to London fifteen years ago, he had a realization: "I'm not talented or even fit enough to play at the level I want to play, so I started investing money and time into becoming a better umpire. And now I travel Europe." He is now the Umpire Director for the British Baseball Federation, holding clinics and providing courses for umpires, as well as supervising tournaments like this one, which features seven umps who are working for the first time. It's always a struggle to convince people to take on the role of umpire because, if they do stay around the game when they finish their playing careers, the normal trajectory runs from player to coach. He points at the field umpire and tells me his name is Alex Deacon and that he's just eighteen. Gabor says, "Alex is really interesting because he is an active player and then he's got this ability to switch from player to umpire, which I think is a very important part of learning to umpire. You have to kill the player in you because you're naturally following the ball." The next time the ball is in play, I follow the line of Alex's gaze, watch the way he keeps his attention on the base he is covering while also keeping the ball in his peripheral vision. As we talk, Croydon continues to pile on the runs. I thank Gabor for his time and walk back to the bleacher behind home plate to watch Ireland's final swings. The game ends 15–0 Croydon.

As I walk back towards Home Plate to check on the other scores in the early games, I notice a group of players in New Forest Thunder Knights uniforms sitting on the stands by the batting cages. New this year, New Forest were one of the teams I considered visiting when I was putting together my itinerary, but I simply could not slot them in to the logistical puzzle. I introduce myself, ask them about the origins of the team and how it's been going in their inaugural season. They tell me that most of them played for the Bournemouth club last year but that they split with them for many reasons, none of which they wished to elaborate on. It's a story I've heard and will hear several times—certainly with the Cork Renegades, but particularly with respect to English baseball—about new clubs forming out of a rift within an existing club or because of internal politics. As Ed Peebles of the Cardiff Merlins will tell me when I mention New Forest, "You find that a lot in the UK—there [are] two clubs quite near each other that started as one club and then they split off because they fell out." Maybe it's just the density of population and the close proximity of population centres that make it easier in England for new teams to form. Maybe it's a historical cycle of rift and reinvention. For whatever reason, this propensity for fragmentation is a ghost that seems to haunt the English game.

Whatever the cause, new beginnings can often be productive, as seen in the success of both the Renegades and the Thunder Knights. Most of the New Forest players are British natives, and there are few expats on the roster. As they began to map out beginnings of the new club, the most difficult aspect was finding a place to play on the South Coast. Player Shaun Barrett tells me, "Even getting a diamond in the UK to be able to play on—that was the first challenge. Once we got there, it was just, 'Let's enjoy this year.'" The club currently play their home games at Southampton University, but like so many other clubs across England, Scotland, and Ireland, they are in the process of trying to find a permanent home. As I listen to the players speak, the talk keeps circling back around to the community they've all found in the team, how they don't mind travelling forty minutes to training. How the more experienced players are good about helping newcomers. How baseball and this team feel so different than previous experiences with competitive sports. How what brings them all together is a love of baseball. This is baseball against the odds. Grassroots baseball—with all its idiosyncrasies and specifics of context—that takes commitment, passion, and belief to keep it going.

As I'm waiting for the start of the Scotland–Liverpool game, Ross Marnie sees me standing on the rise behind their dugout. He waves and trots over, hands me an airplane-sized bottle of Scotch. The Baseball Scotland logo dominates the label atop words that read, *Baseball Scotland Team Farnham July 22/23 2023*. Gifts for the teams they will play this weekend. I tell Ross that I'm pleased to receive one. He smiles and heads back to his teammates while I take a seat with the Ireland players behind home plate.

We watch a strong opening inning for the Trojans, their hitters pounding the ball and taking a quick 4–0 lead. On seeing a fielding error, Pedro leans over to me, nods toward third, and jokes that it's hard to play the field here because he keeps expecting the bad hops of Corkagh. He's probably right that few here this weekend have played on infields as well-groomed as these.

Scotland comes back to score two in the bottom half of the first to make it 4–2, a score which still holds in the top of the third when I and almost all the spectators retreat from the heavy rain that has started to fall. Back at Home Plate, along with virtually everyone not currently playing, I meet Brendan Power, one of the first players anyone mentioned to me when I started thinking about this project and one of the only connections between baseball in the Windsor (Ontario, not England) area—where he played for the Tecumseh Thunder—and baseball in Ireland and the UK. Shoulder-length hair trails out of the back of his cap, and there's a few days' growth to his beard. He's compact, an infielder with powerful forearms who has kept himself in playing shape as he has moved into his thirties. He's here this weekend with the London Mets, the team he's been playing with for years since moving to London (England, not Ontario), where he teaches biology and physical education. In his seventh season, he now manages the Mets, taking the place of the club's previous manager, Drew Spencer, who now manages the Great Britain National Team. The move, he says, has broadened his perspective on the game. Like others I've met, he sees the importance of getting kids into the sport and he's been trying to get baseball into the schools around London, but it's an uphill battle, especially since there is such little space to carve out a place to play in the inner city. We talk a bit about Windsor, about shared acquaintances, before he moves off to be with his teammates. I drink another cup of coffee and wait for the rain to subside.

Eventually the rain lightens enough for me to trudge back to the Scotland–Liverpool game. They have played through the deluge under conditions that have been, shall we say, less than ideal. I move in to stand behind the backstop, next to where Ewan Spence—decked out in full kilt—keeps score for Scotland. I ask him where we're at, and he tells me that it's the bottom of the fifth and there is one out, with the score 6–3 Liverpool. The bases are loaded, but the two-hour time limit is becoming a factor for Scotland. It's a favourable count for the hitter as the rain continues to fall. There's lots of encouragement from the Scotland bench, and a cheer goes up as a walk scores a run to make the score 6–4, but there are only a few minutes until the game will be called for time. Top of the order with the ballgame on the line. Evaldas Grinys, who plays for the Glasgow Galaxy, comes to the plate. From the Scotland bench come cries of encouragement. "All you, baby, all you. Come on, Elvis, you're in the driving seat." He fouls off a couple of tough pitches, works the count to 3–2. From the dugout you can hear cries of "Nobody better. Come on." A seven-pitch walk scores another run and the score is 6–5.

That brings up left-handed hitter Jared Thomley. Behind me, the Long Eaton and Ireland teams watch the unfolding drama as the clock ticks toward the end of the game. On a 2–1 pitch, Thornley singles, but the ball only makes its way far enough past the infield to score one run. The game is tied at 6 as Miguel Del Rosario of the Edinburgh Cannons, one of the best hitters on the Scotland team, steps to the plate. Three minutes until time will be called on this game. Foul. Foul. Foul. From the bench Paul Convoy, the Scotland manager yells, "Two minutes, guys! Two minutes!" They're now playing as much against the clock as they are against Liverpool. On the 0–2 pitch, Miguel reaches and hits a towering foul ball out of play just beyond the backstop and the catcher's glove. Another 0–2 pitch, but this time he manages to square up the ball for a walk-off single. Scotland win the game in five innings, beating both Liverpool and the game clock. The rain that's been steadily falling starts coming down even harder as players and spectators alike scramble for the shelter of Home Plate.

The rain keeps on and on, sometimes seeming to lighten but never completely abating. As long as there is rain, they won't start the next set of games. The players crowd into the small pub and the tent-covered patio next door, sometimes greeting people they know from other teams. Some are former teammates, others players they have encountered often, a few people they recognize from other tournaments. The baseball world here is, after all, small. For the most part, though, the teams stick with each other, making the best they can of the delay. Some are clearly enjoying themselves, their boisterous conversation and laughter filling their corner of the patio, while others stand by the window or the open door and stare at the seemingly unending rain.

I step outside to get some air. The rain is much lighter, though still steady. Next to me, a couple of players are also craning their necks toward the sky, trying to ascertain whether or not there might be any baseball today. One of them wears a Cardiff Merlins jersey, so I introduce myself, tell him that it's the next stop on this summer's baseball trip. He tells me his name is Nick South and that he is the manager of the Merlins I team. He knows who I am from my correspondence with Andrew Snow and Ed Peebles, and he tells me that they are looking forward to hosting me in Cardiff. We talk a bit about the tournament, the conversation always circling back to the weather and what it will mean not only for today, but also for the games tomorrow. Nick stares into the distance, tells me that the weather is by far the biggest factor with which they contend in trying to play baseball in England and in Wales, and that they often play in the kind of rain that's coming down right now. It won't be the last time someone says that or the last time weather intrudes on this trip.

Back in the tent, I'm finally able to catch up with Paul Convoy, President of Baseball Scotland. We've been corresponding for several months, but kept missing each other during my time in Scotland. He is a man of great girth and full beard, with a booming and ever-present laugh that sometimes causes his glasses to slide down his nose. Paul tells me that he's been involved in baseball now for seventeen years, making the move over from the softball he had played in Dundee. He first played baseball with the now-defunct Edinburgh Giants, transitioning first to on-field manager, then taking over the running of the club, and eventually becoming head of the league and of Baseball Scotland. Here he laughs and says, "It's been a gradual progression in leadership." He first got interested in baseball through watching Major League games late at night in the early 2000s. This was MLB on Five, the live broadcasts of games that Channel 5 ran from 1997 to 2008, featuring now legendary Anglo-American broadcaster Josh Chetwynd. It is not the first—nor will it be the last—time that someone has told me that this was their introduction to baseball. Going to a game in Philadelphia, though, was where Paul really "caught the bug," as he says. "The whole vibe of the place made me fall in love with the sport." I ask him what it is about baseball that has captured and sustained his interest. What he tells me revises the oft-stated notion that baseball is a sport that is *about* failure: "To me, you won't get a much more team sport than baseball. Everybody's got a different role. Everybody has to do it well. If you don't do it well, you get another chance at it. There's no such thing as failure in baseball. There's always the next pitch. There's always the next play."

According to Paul, the Slough tournament is a chance to bring the Scottish National League together, to reinforce the notion that they are all trying to move collectively in the same direction even while they are doing the work in their own clubs. And the club level is, he asserts, where it all starts, the foundation for Baseball Scotland. It does not work "unless you have someone there who's willing to do the graft and the time that's required—and it's a massive ask." In words that echo what Sean Mitchell told me a few weeks ago, Paul goes on to say that clubs start and die when the right people aren't there. Fortunately, there are good people in place at the current clubs, people committed to the idea and the reality of baseball in Scotland. I ask him about that idea of Scottish baseball, and he replies, "It's being competitive, but having fun. It's having fun and learning and developing. It's learning and developing and trying something new."

The biggest challenge is the lack of facilities, a sentiment that echoes what I've seen throughout my travels. In Paul's mind, getting a proper diamond in every city is the first step towards growing the game. The second part of the equation is developing youth baseball, but that, again, comes back to the availability of volunteers. Paul tries to delegate, but while he has good people on the ground at all of the clubs, there just aren't enough people to do the work, a fact that's difficult to remedy. "We're all working together to make the best situation for everybody," Paul says. "If you're not working together and pulling in the same direction, it can fall apart."

Paul tells me I should speak with Fiona Brambley, Baseball Scotland's social media coordinator, one of the people who, along with those on the ground at the clubs, helps with the heavy workload of keeping things running. Paul calls over to Fiona and introduces us. I ask her about doing social media for the league, and she tells me that despite the fact that it's hard to keep up with everything, at Glasgow, her home club, social media has helped them increase their number from around forty members to their current seventy, including both those who play in games and those who come out only for training. It's a base to which they hope to add a youth program in the future as a way to further grow the club, a plan which depends on getting volunteer coaches in place.

She herself has been playing since 2019, though she had been familiar with the sport since encountering it in France, where she is from originally, in 2012. In an accent that to me sounds completely Scottish, she says, "I came across one of my now teammates in Tesco with a baseball bat sticking out of his bag, and I says, 'Do you play baseball?' And he says, 'Yeah, I do.' So that's how I got into it." Last year, Fiona trained with the Great Britain Women's National Team and has recently played with the Glasgow Sunflowers, a new women's team that she says was inspired in part by the recent *A League of Their Own* television adaptation. "They already have over fifty members—it's a lot of girls [and] members of the LGBTQ community—who are keen to try something different. And they absolutely love it." In their first game, against the Leicester Diamonds, who I will be meeting in a couple of weeks, the Sunflowers had a hundred people out to watch.

I ask her about learning to play baseball as an adult. She chuckles and says, "It's strange because there are so many rules. So I'm learning every single time. The Glasgow club [is] really good and encouraging. I do enjoy watching games as well. I'm just trying to take in everything that I can. I know I'm not going to be the best player in Scotland, but just as long as I enjoy it, I think that's the main thing." Later she says, "It's good fun. That's the thing about playing baseball to me—everyone's just there to have a good time."

The day is finally called just before four p.m. with the completion of only the first two game slots. There is no word on the plan or schedule for tomorrow. The parking lot begins to empty as players depart. I see the Irish contingent gathered near where the road enters the parking lot. They've called for a couple of Ubers and ask if I need a ride back to my hotel. I quickly accept, grateful to not have to wait for the bus which now runs only once an hour.

The vehicles arrive, and I pile into a van with Jason, Sean, Vanessa, Chris, Feidhlim, and Ryan. As the van heads south towards town, there's a lot of talk about how they could have played, how they've played through much worse weather than was seen today. It's nothing I hadn't heard in the tent, but the Cup organizers were adamant that they would not start a game while it was raining. Continue, yes. Start, no.

I ask Sean if he has heard anything else, but he says they won't really know much until later this evening. The one thing they do know is that they will likely not have to play at eight a.m., in what will now be the first slot of the day, since there are teams who were not able to take the field at all today. Ireland and Scotland can unwind tonight knowing that they probably will not play before the ten a.m. slot. When I say goodbye to Feidhlim and Ryan, the three of us the last to be dropped off, I tell them that I might see them later at The Moon and Spoon.

SUNDAY, JULY 23, 2023

The next morning, I catch the nine a.m. bus to Farnham, opting for much-needed sleep over the slate of eight a.m. games that feature the ten teams who did not play yesterday. These are the first of what are now all termed playoff games, with winners and losers then sorted into the appropriate bracket. A single loss, either yesterday or in these early games, would mean that the team could not win its division championship, but would instead play to get into the third-place contest. Games will now be capped at one hour and forty-five minutes, with no new innings starting after one hour and thirty minutes, and these games will position teams from first to eighth in each division. Scotland still has a chance at winning the Gold championship, while Ireland can now only hope for third place. It's not an ideal scenario, but in a two-day tournament, there isn't much room to revise when the weather doesn't cooperate.

I drift over to one of the back diamonds, hoping to catch the end of Norwich Iceni–University of Nottingham, a game in the Silver Division. It's already 12–1 for Norwich after three innings, despite there being a five run per inning cap in games in the Silver and Bronze Divisions. The Norwich team should be coming off the field for the top of the fourth, but instead the pitcher re-sets and awaits another hitter to take their position in the batter's box. I ask the scorekeeper what's happening, and he tells me that they're using the "Follow-on" rule, in which the losing team bats again if the other team is at least seven runs up when the final inning is called. It's a rule that's been used for a few years in leagues in the east of England and has been adopted for this tournament. A wrinkle in the rules that is certainly new to me.

The Nottingham team does manage to score one more run and perhaps would have had another but for a very nice play by the Norwich pitcher, who goes to his left to corral a ground ball and then throws to first for the out. When the game ends, I ask the university players if I might talk to one of them about the team, and they volunteer their captain, Alex Uner. I'm interested in who comes out for uni baseball, and he tells me that ninety percent of the team is new players—true, he thinks, for most university teams—and that many of them are former or current cricketers. They get recruits through club days, flyers, social media, and any other exposure they can get to new students. Only a few keep playing after university, and that decision is often a function of where they decide to live after graduation and whether or not there is a team there. As a university team, they don't get much chance at actual games. As Alex puts it, "Our season runs basically from October to March. We play very few games, and those we do play are pretty miserable. So we saw an opportunity to come and play—we love playing here because we don't get a lot of opportunities to play on an actual baseball field." I thank Alex and wave goodbye to the rest of the team, seeing now why they've come to Slough. Seeing now that playing on an actual diamond, rather than on a grass field with no mound, is a rare privilege for them.

The sun is shining and there is no rain in the forecast as I make my way to the Ireland–BC Vetra game. Players from the London Mets and the Essex Baseball Club huddle against the howling wind, gathering themselves for the games they will play at noon against Croydon and Scotland for berths in the Gold Division championship game. They speak to each other in low tones, watching as BC Vetra gets ready to take the field for the first inning. The BC Vetra players are much older than their opponents today, with most in their thirties and some in their forties, but almost all are powerfully built. Some look like more like weightlifters than they do ballplayers. From Bristol, the team has a large contingent of players originally from Lithuania, along with a number of Latin American expats. Under the new tournament format, they are in this game as a result of their first-day loss to the Mets.

In the first inning, Ireland puts runners on the corners with two outs but are unable to score a run. Jeremy O'Brien takes the mound for Ireland in the bottom of the inning. It's a shaky start as he gives up two walks and unleashes a wild pitch before committing a balk to make the score 1–0 for BC Vetra. But then he is able to settle down, recording three outs in succession on a pop-up to third base, a strikeout, and a ground ball to third base. From the berm behind me, I hear Steve Silverberg's distinctive New York accent as he tells his gathered teammates, "We came here to face the best. Let's fucking do it."

Ireland comes to life in the second inning when Ryan Wiebe doubles to score runners from second and third. 2–1 Ireland. Three consecutive walks score a third run and chase the BC Vetra starting pitcher from the game. It's a big inning that might have been even bigger but for a spectacular play by the catcher on a pop-up, as he slides and gathers the ball into his glove in foul territory along the third baseline. The bases are left loaded, and BC Vetra are able to close the gap to 3–2 when they score a run in the bottom half of the inning on a walk, wild pitch, passed ball, and groundout to short.

Each team puts men on base in the third, but neither is able to push a run across, keeping the score 3–2 Ireland entering the fourth and final inning. With one out in the top of the inning, David Linn makes good contact on a ball that keeps rolling in the outfield, allowing him to race around the bases for a triple. But with Matt Dutton at the plate, David takes off for home and is tagged out. Did Matt miss the sign for a hit and run? Was the squeeze on? Did David miss the sign, running when he should have just taken a good secondary lead? Whatever the reason, Ireland squander a golden opportunity for an important insurance run. BC Vetra come to bat in the bottom of the game's final inning.

The first hitter reaches on an error, while the second is hit by a pitch. A passed ball moves the runners up to second and third, and a wild pitch scores the tying run. Strikeout. Runner on third with one out. Patrick Mitchell in to pitch. As he toes the rubber, I wonder how his stuff will play after pitching a couple of innings yesterday. But before I can even really think about what the pitch sequence might look like, the runner is charging home from third for the winning run. A passed ball? A wild pitch? It happened so fast that I'm not able to score the play accurately, just able to note that it's one among many unforced errors in an inning that sees BC Vetra score two runs without the benefit of a hit.

While I await the start of the Scotland–Essex game, I strike up a conversation with Davey Fair, who is sitting on the bleachers now as his teammates make their preparations for the game. He'll be in the dugout for the game itself, but since he was injured in the Tayport intrasquad game, he is resting here until the game is ready to begin. He grew up in Scotland, but he has been playing since he was a kid, taking up the game when he visited Toronto in the summers with his family. He then played on a junior team in Dundee, back when there was a youth league, and had the opportunity to attend the Great Britain Cadets (U15) camp when he was fifteen. He even played a bit with the Great Britain U18 team. After that, he played in Edinburgh for a few years and at one point was offered a partial scholarship to play baseball at a junior college in the US, but couldn't afford to go. Eventually, he retired, taking ten years off before coming back to the game when the Tayport club formed. There's a twinkle in his eye when he tells me, "I've got a little bit of time left." Initially, he played first base because of issues with his back, but when Paul Gardner and Tom Knox joined in the second year, there were suddenly three first basemen on the roster. Paul ended up at third base and Davey behind the plate, the position he had primarily played when coming up as a junior. Before he walks over to the dugout for the start of the game, he looks up at me and says, "I'm not gonna give up. I'm at least gonna get another few years."

Starting today for Scotland is Hsinyen Lai, who takes the mound in the bottom of the first inning after Scotland strands a runner and fails to score in the top half of the inning. The first batter lines out to short, but a single and a triple result in the first run of the game. As the rally mounts, there's lots of animated encouragement—mostly in Spanish—from the Essex dugout. A sacrifice fly to right field then makes it 2–0 before a pop-up to the catcher ends the inning. Scotland has work to do as they come to the plate in the second inning. There's one out when they put runners on second and third through a single, hit batter, and passed ball. F1 for out number two, a notation that does not do justice to what a great catch the pitcher makes in foul territory as he races from the mound and slides past the third baseline to snare the ball. A walk to load the bases, but the inning ends on a pop to short. Still 2–0 Essex going into the bottom of the second inning.

Essex opens its half with a single. From the Scotland bench someone yells, "Let's go, professor!" Hsinyen settles himself, inducing a fly ball to left field and a ball straight back to the mound. He walks the next batter, but another fly ball to left field gets him out of the inning. As they come off the field, I hear from the Scotland bench, "2-3-4. Smells like runs!"

Scotland gets a runner aboard when leadoff hitter Jared Thomley singles up the middle. Miguel Del Rosario then hits a towering fly ball, but the right fielder tracks it down for the second out, bringing Ren Quantrill from the Edinburgh Cannons to the plate. From my place directly behind the Scotland bench, I hear, "Fastball, fastball. Curveball when he's ahead." Ren scorches the ball between second and third, but the Essex shortstop, Luke Foley, dives to his right and snares it in the outer webbing of his glove before landing hard on the grass. It's a defensive gem and easily the best play I've seen on this trip.

Scotland manage to score only once in the inning, when Tom Knox singles and the ball is overthrown in an attempt to get Ren out at third. In the bottom of the inning, a combination of hits and errors plates three more runs for Essex, a result that could have been worse if not for a stellar diving catch by Paul Gardner. The umpires signal that an hour and a half has elapsed, so the next inning will be the last. One final shot for Scotland in the fourth inning.

Peter Rowe, the designated hitter, leads off and reaches base when he beats out an infield single, moving to second on a balk. That brings up Paul Gardner, who also hits an infield single to put runners on the corners. A run scores on the overthrow to second on Paul's steal. 5–2 Essex. Strikeout for the first out. You can feel the tension from the Scotland bench, the nervousness in the way they shout encouragement to their teammates. "Find a way! All you. Come on 1!" A ground ball to second base brings Scotland to its final out. Jared singles to cut the lead to 5–3, but that's all Scotland can manage in this truncated game. They will play the loser of the London Mets–Croydon Pirates game.

I spend the afternoon wandering from diamond to diamond, taking in snatches of various games. On one of the back diamonds, I catch the end of the Mets–Pirates game, with the Pirates unable to score in their final at-bats, losing 3–1 to the Mets. On a temporary field, marked off in the outfield by orange fencing that lists in the wind, I watch an inning of a Bronze Division game between the Stockton Grizzlies and the Fire Breathing Kittens, a team made up of players from the East of England Baseball League. With Gabriel Fidler, a journalist who writes about baseball in the UK as well as in other countries, I see part of a Silver Division game between the Bristol Bats and the Bracknell Inferno. We've had several conversations over the weeks leading up to my trip, but this is the first time I've met Gabriel. As we talk about the tournament, he snaps photos of the game action, tells me that he will be one of the broadcasters for the Gold Division final, with the feed going out over the internet through BBF's social media channels. I ask about the broadcast, and he tells me that it's early days so they're still working the kinks out. The hope is that streaming will mean some exposure, a sentiment much like that expressed early in the trip by Brett Sutherland in Cork. He asks what I've seen on my travels, and we chat amiably about grassroots baseball culture here, in Scotland, and in Ireland, and everything it entails.

As I fetch a cup of coffee and make my way over to see the end of the Ireland–Sheffield Bruins game, I find myself thinking once more about all the people it takes to make baseball run here, to make a tournament like this one run. Organizers. Players. Coaches. Umpires. Scorekeepers. Journalists like Gabriel. Or photographers like John Linton, who is here with Baseball Scotland. Everyone here because they love this niche sport.

As I walk up, I see Jeremy double to left centre, scoring Feidhlim and moving Pedro to third base. I spot Jason behind the Ireland bench and ask him what's up with the game. He tells me that the score was 1–1 after the first inning, but that this run now makes it 14–1 in the top of the second inning. The umpires have already called the final inning, which means that if they are not able to finish, the game will revert to the score at the end of the first. I watch as Pedro plants himself down the third baseline in an attempt to give himself up for the final out. Instead, the Sheffield pitcher balks and Pedro trots home to make the score 15–1. After Jeremy moves to third base on the balk, he stands three feet past the base until the third baseman finally tags him out. The game ends on two groundouts and a strikeout from Sheffield in the bottom of the second inning.

The final games of the day are the championships for each division. For the Gold Division, it's the Mets and Essex. These are two of the best clubs in the UK, and both teams are fielding a mix of players from their AAA and National

Baseball League teams, so it should be a very good game. Luke Foley strides to the plate to start the first inning for Essex, singling past the shortstop on the second pitch of the game. He takes an aggressive lead and breaks for second but is thrown out on a strong throw from Joshua Barrett. I've become so used to steals being nearly automatic in these games that I star the play in my notes. A strikeout and fly to right field end the Essex half of the first inning.

Jake Turtel singles to left to lead off the inning for the Mets. Giovanni Pappalardo throws over to first once, twice, three times. I can't help but think of the new MLB rules and how the third throw over has to result in an out or the runner is awarded second base. Not here. It turns out it doesn't matter when a walk to Lee Cameron puts two runners on base. A promising start to the inning, but it all comes to nought as the next three batters fail to get a hit. No score at the end of one inning.

The lead runner is once more aboard for Essex when Angel Pérez singles through the left side. Franklin Martínez walks. Runners on first and second. A steal of third and a strikeout mean runners on the corners with one out. With Giovanni Escalona at the plate, Martínez takes off for second, and when the Mets throw through, Pérez breaks for home on a delayed steal and is called safe for the first run of the game. They add another on a fielding error by the Mets to make the score 2–0 Essex. In their half of the inning, the Mets score a run on three consecutive singles from Joshua Barrett, Johan Villanueva, and Mitchell vom Scheidt, but also leave the bases loaded, a golden opportunity with only one out squandered. 2–1 Essex after two innings.

There is no scoring in the third thanks to solid defence from both sides, including a pickoff and run-down between third base and home in the top of the inning and a nice play by the catcher on a swinging bunt in the bottom of the inning. As I watch, I see that Scotland are playing Croydon on the diamond to my right. Beyond, Ireland have picked up an exhibition game against Bracknell.

Essex put a man on in the top of the fourth, but cannot bring home the badly needed insurance run. Mets up in their half, with time ticking towards the hour and a half mark, at which point the final inning will be called. With one out, Turtel singles past the pitcher to put the tying run on base. On the first pitch of the next at-bat, Turtel steals second base, scoring one pitch later on a throwing error by the third baseman. He's exuberant as he scores, jumping wildly at the plate, greeting his teammates with a blur of high fives. The Bournemouth players who are sitting behind the play try to get his attention, chanting in unison, "62! 62! We love you, 62!" The Mets score the go-ahead run when Dylan Baxter singles to plate Lee Cameron who had reached on the error that scored Turtel. 3–2 Mets.

The ump announces that we're just under the hour and a half mark—perhaps even in the final minute—and so there will be a fifth inning, a final chance for Essex to come back. As he did in the first, Foley gets things started with a single. On the first pitch of his at-bat, Gálvez Rodríguez bunts, and it takes a very good play from the pitcher to get him at first base, but it does move Foley up to second base. Next up is Yonathan Novas, who hits a chopper to between first and second that takes a bad hop before being deftly fielded by the second baseman for the second out. Foley to third base, just ninety feet from tying the game. The Mets opt to intentionally walk Pérez, bringing Franklin Martínez to the plate with runners on the corners. But Martínez does not see a single pitch as Pérez gets hung up between first and second on a pickoff throw from the pitcher and is tagged out at second before Foley can cross the plate. The Mets are champions of the Gold Division of the BBF Summer Cup. It was, as I hoped, a very well-played game and a nice glimpse at the standard of play in the highest level of baseball in the UK.

I share an Uber back to Slough with Gabriel, and we talk a bit about the tournament, about what we've seen. It was hard competition, but with stakes that seemed much lower than almost every tournament I've attended in North America. More than that, though, it always seemed to be just as much about fun and the chance to play the game on good fields. Before we left Farnham Park, Feidhlim told me that the game against Bracknell was just fun, a game with absolutely no pressure. And this idea of fun was even more pronounced as I watched Silver and, particularly, Bronze Division games. Except for the very top teams, there is no real chance of any higher stakes, so you need to enjoy what's on offer. Everyone involved takes the games seriously, but at the end of the day, they all know it's a game and that it's supposed to be fun. Their passion and commitment are to baseball for its own sake. For those involved here, baseball often seems to capture people and really get under their skin. Baseball is baseball, yes, but it wouldn't happen here without all of these people and their passion and commitment and belief, which are the engines that keep baseball going here where all the odds seem to be stacked against it.

We're both silent for a moment as the English countryside spools past the car before we turn onto a city street that takes us to my hotel. We shake hands, and Gabriel departs for the train station a block to the north. I turn to enter the hotel, eager to hear about Heidi's weekend. Tomorrow morning, we board the train for Cardiff.

CARDIFF

> I just love the fact that you become good friends with people that you would never have met if it wasn't for baseball.
>
> —ED PEEBLES, CARDIFF MERLINS

TUESDAY, JULY 25, 2023

I latch the garden gate of our current flat, slip on my headphones, and start to walk. Right on Cowbridge, tracing the commercial heart of Canton as I walk towards Pontcanna Fields for tonight's Cardiff Merlins training session. Smokers loiter outside the Clive Arms. The last customers of the day slouch out of the Turkish barber. Charity shops turn signs from *OPEN* to *CLOSED*. People wander in to various shops to get their takeaways for the evening. Near the Tesco at Clive Road, I cut north, leaving behind the shops and the bustle of Cowbridge. Rowhouses line both sides of the road, people behind the doors at their dinners or unwinding after a long day at work. By the time I get to Pencisely Road, the houses have become larger, more updated. I turn right and the housing turns stately along Pencisely in the blocks that lead to where it becomes Penhill Road at the point Llandaff Fields begin. I opt not to cross this park that butts up against Pontcanna, but instead stay on the city streets so that I can enter near the parking lot off Fields Park Road, the route that seems most likely for players to take from their cars to the field.

Next to the parking lot sits a squat, single-storey brick building with the words *Capital for Sport* painted across its right half in large white cursive, bracketed by the Welsh words *Caerdydd* and *Prifddinas Chwaraeon* in smaller red lettering. The left half of the building is taken up with murals of Welsh athletes. I recognize Gareth Bale at the far left, but the others, including a track athlete, rugby player, and wheelchair racer are unknown to me. All are men. Sports centre or changing rooms, this building is clearly connected in some way to the playing fields beyond.

To the left of this building, I see a path that leads into Pontcanna. Once again, I don't know exactly where the baseball field is located within the larger park, but it's not quite six p.m. and I have time to get the lay of the land before training begins. I follow the path in and to the right until I get to a walkway that bisects the park, dividing it into two larger sections that can accommodate multiple activities across their large, open spaces. As I walk, I'm enclosed by trees on either side, the canopy of leaves shading me from the evening's sun. Through the breaks in the trees, I see people running, both alone and in pairs. A football team in a circle tries to keep the ball in the air. A dog chases a ball. A group of teenagers lounges on the grass. A cricketer puts the flat of his bat on a bouncing ball. Behind me, a bicycle rings its bell to pass.

To my left, across the wide expanse of grass, I finally see the shape of a baseball diamond. There is no backstop or permanent fencing, but the outlines of the field are clearly marked—cutouts for bases, a permanent mound, white baselines extending from home plate to the arc of the perimeter line that marks the edge of the outfield. I make my way to where the backstop would be, shrug off my backpack, and sit down on the grass to wait for the Merlins to arrive. A couple of South Asian families—several adults and kids—walk straight across second base and the mound itself before seeing me and veering towards third base. One of the adults kicks a soccer ball, while the other adults are in deep conversation. The kids laugh as they chase each other. It's clear that none of them have any idea what the marks on the field might be or why there are patches of dirt on an otherwise pristine stretch of grass. They are simply out for a walk on a summer evening in late July.

The family fades into the distance, replaced by crows that hop around the space between first and second base. I check my watch. Six p.m. Time for the players to begin arriving. The Merlins field two teams, both at the A level, and have about forty people on their combined roster, plus another ten or so who train but do not play. The Merlins I team was slated to go up to AA this year, but have not done so, opting to stay instead in the Single-A South West & Wales Baseball League, along with Merlins II, Bournemouth Bears, Bristol Brunels, Bristol Buccaneers, Cornish Claycutters, New Forest Thunder Knights, Taunton Muskets, and Weston Jets. There is no doubt that they would be competitive in AA, having shown themselves to be the best team in the SWWBL for the past couple of years. The problem, as will soon be explained to me, lies in the fact that they are at the far reaches of baseball in the southwest of the UK, especially in relation to greater London, the area from which many of the AA teams are drawn. On a practical level, staying in their current league ensures that they will get more games. The hope is that in the 2024 season there may be enough teams for a smaller AA league closer by, as some of the current league clubs become able to field more than one team. But that remains to be seen.

Players begin to appear, singly and in pairs. One of them shepherds a cart of equipment from the canopied path across the grass to the diamond. A slender, clean-shaven man walks over and introduces himself as Ed Peebles, my main contact with the club in the weeks leading up to the trip. He tells me that he needs to get the practice started, but that he'll have time to talk a bit later. In the meantime, he introduces me to Steve Smith, who took on the role of manager of the Merlins II team in 2022. Unfortunately, his counterpart with Merlins I, Nick South, who I met in Slough, won't be here tonight, but should be at the scheduled league game on Sunday afternoon.

Steve is older, in his early fifties, and the physical opposite of Ed—short, stocky, with a full salt-and-pepper beard beneath sunglasses and a black ball cap. He grew up in Erie, Pennsylvania, playing baseball until he was fifteen or sixteen before picking it up again when he came to the UK for his PhD in 2001. It has been, he says, "a nice little hobby of home kind of thing." He played in both Manchester and Birmingham before taking a job at Cardiff University in 2016, the year the Merlins were formed. When he first came to the UK, he played middle infield, but now when he plays it's at first base. But he mainly manages, working with the newer players that make up Merlins II. It's a way to stay involved, to keep that piece of home at hand.

The players are mostly British, with a few expats thrown in. When I ask about managing, Steve replies that it's "fun, but frustrating at times." He goes on to say that all the things that are ingrained if you've played since you were a kid are not second nature to the adults playing here. For example, it is often difficult for players to recognize what to do when fielding a ball at either a high or low trajectory because of "the inability to realize when you flip the glove over." What would be second nature to someone who grew up with the game involves conscious thought rather than reflexive action, indecision that often leads to errors on the field.

There are about twenty-five or so players here for tonight's session. Ed has finished leading them through the ritual of stretches and jogging around the outfield, and now has about half the team doing outfield drills and the other half infield drills, while individual players wander in for soft toss swings into the net. I watch him take a couple of ground balls, moving his body so he's squarely in front of it, trying to anticipate any bad hop that might occur. He watches what I assume must be a new player taking a similar ground ball and says a few words about bending the knees, being ready to move in any direction. He smiles and nods when the player successfully fields a second ball, cushioning it into his glove before making an awkward throw to first. One step at a time.

Ed looks to the outfield to check on their progress, and when he seems satisfied he makes his way over to me. Like many others, he got into the game through watching MLB on Five late at night in the early 2000s. He played a year of baseball in Bristol in 2014, but then subsequently played softball in Cardiff. The Merlins grew out of softball, much in the way baseball started thirty years ago in Ireland. Ed and Ben Kwiatkowski were two of the principal founders of the club in 2018, which served as a development year before they joined the league in 2019. Ed was, he maintains, "only playing softball because I couldn't play baseball because there was no team. When I was playing softball, in my mind I was playing baseball." Those who wanted to play baseball had no choice but to take the reins and do it for themselves, and Ed was one of the prime movers. Officially the club's treasurer, he remains the person who is tasked with most of the day-to-day work necessary for "keeping the club ticking over."

Exclusively an adult team, the Merlins try to "look for guys coming across from other sports—especially cricket, but also field hockey and ice hockey, football, rugby" because they see the skills as transferable, while the rules of the game can be learned. Players from sports like rugby see baseball as a way to stay active without the same risk of injury. They also search for players who grew up playing elsewhere and have now moved to Cardiff, such as Saliya Wijesinghe, who played for the Sri Lankan National Team and is currently the main starter for Merlins I. Much of the success of Merlins I comes down to having pitchers like Saliya who can throw strikes since, as Steve tells me, at this level "everybody has a hole in their swing." For the most part, however, the Merlins know that they need to recruit players new to the sport. I ask Ed how he sells the game to them. His reply is that "you don't need to be super fit. It's a skill-based game—you know, throwing, catching, hitting. If you've got some basic ability, there is a spot on the field for you." One of the main advantages they have in recruitment lies in the fact that they are the only team in Wales, the only team around. "It has the advantage that we get everyone who wants to play baseball. We've basically got a huge catchment area all to ourselves." The downside, of course, is that they have travel times as long as three or four hours to away games.

Funding for the club comes mainly from membership dues—currently £120 per year—and a small amount of sponsorship from local companies. The diamond here is part of the larger public park that is Pontcanna Fields and, as I suspected, does not belong to them. That means that people are constantly riding across the field and it is impossible for them to leave any equipment out. Even attempting to cover the mound—in place only since 2021—has proven impossible, as Ed tells me, saying, "Somebody's nicked the tarp," a phrase I hear repeated several times over the course of the evening. Setup for games takes so much time that even home games require all-day commitment from the players. As I've heard often on this trip, their hope is to fully enclose the field and lease it from the Cardiff Council so that they have full control over it. In the meantime, they are hesitant to even erect a backstop because of the expectation of vandalism.

I ask Ed and Steve about the league and the relationship between it and the British Baseball Federation as none of it appears to be as straightforward as it is in either Ireland or Scotland. They look at each other in a way that indicates it's a long story. This league, Ed tells me, is now affiliated with the BBF, but it was independent when they joined in 2019. That year there was a schism between those who wanted to be in the BBF, those who didn't, and those who wanted something in between. Ed says, "So much politics—you've probably heard this from other teams. It's ridiculous. It's so complicated, and you'd think everyone would be pulling in the same direction. It's because it's a small world, everyone has their little thing and people want to be in charge of stuff." As this point, Steve interjects: "I will say it's been that way for twenty years. When I started in Manchester, which was one of the big clubs in the north, the politics of all that nonsense went on for a few years." He pauses. "It's a game of baseball. Just go play baseball."

The league as currently constructed is independent—it sets its own fixtures and produces its own champion—but is also technically within the BBF structure, what Ed calls "officially affiliated" but with "a measure of autonomy." It's a structure that both Ed and Steve think would make sense for other leagues to adopt as well and is potentially a way forward for British baseball.

We talk a bit about Welsh baseball, a game something like stickball that was historically played in Cardiff, Newport, and

Liverpool. There is a women's league for Welsh baseball, but there is no interaction between it and the Merlins, especially since the Merlins do not want to be seen as trying to poach their players. I ask about baseball programs for kids in Cardiff, and they mention RBI Wales, an organization affiliated with MLB's "Reviving Baseball in the Inner Cities" program, and Holly Ireland, a name I've now heard several times. Ed says, "We started as an adult team, and because Holly is doing RBI Wales, we kind of leave that to her." I ask about how they can make the club sustainable without a youth program, and he replies, "We really want more guys eighteen, nineteen, and twenty years old, because what we don't want is for the team to go for like ten or fifteen years and then when the founding members go, the team folds, which does happen. We want to create something that will actually last beyond us to the point where maybe we're just managing and not playing."

Training is coming to an end, so I thank Ed and ask if he can suggest a couple of players with whom I might speak after the session. Without hesitation he suggests Jimmy Forsythe and Martin Legge, both in their thirties but with different baseball stories. Jimmy is a former rugby player and one of the founding members of the Merlins. He came to the game through softball, though like the other team founders, he really wanted to play baseball. Having always played a sport, Jimmy felt he needed to transition to something less taxing when his body could no longer handle rugby: "I just think I need something outside of work. I've always done something, so I think I get really twitchy if I haven't done anything outside. I spend more time outside with baseball than I ever did with rugby." Martin, on the other hand, first played baseball twenty years ago in the Bournemouth youth program when he was eleven or twelve, then again for about eighteen months ten years ago.

He came to the Merlins after he started watching baseball again three years ago. The sport came back to him quite quickly, he thinks, because of the time he spent playing it as a kid: "I think if you start young, it obviously drills stuff into you. Starting young certainly gives you a good base."

Both have experimented with multiple positions, something encouraged and perhaps even part of the fabric of the club, as Martin explains, "Everyone—from the first session—is so welcoming. There's nothing cliquey about it. Everyone's very accepting of everyone else's ability. It's fantastic. Every position you want to play, they'll let you have a go at it." As a result, Martin has tried his hand at catching, while Jimmy has started to pitch. Both see these possibilities for individual development as a vital part of what the Merlins offer, along with the mutual support that goes along with it. As Martin puts it, "Everyone is so friendly and helpful to one another." Jimmy echoes this sentiment, though in much more blunt terms, telling me, "We don't seem to attract dickheads."

With games taking up most of a Sunday and training taking place on both Tuesday evenings and Saturday mornings, playing baseball is a large commitment. Plus they, like virtually every other team I've met on this trip, work out in a gym over the winter, taking only a short break between the end of October when the season ends and early January when indoor training begins. What brings them back week after week is not only individual development and camaraderie, but also the fact that baseball is *not* a popular sport. Despite the focus on growth in the many conversations I've had with people over the past few weeks, this latter feeling has also bubbled below the surface, a sentiment that Martin clearly articulates: "I think it's because it's something different as well. I think that's what it is—the nicheness of it, in this country at least. I think that's probably what's drawn me in and kept me interested." The very thing that makes the game precarious is also part of its appeal.

FRIDAY, JULY 28, 2023

Inside Coffee #1, just off Cathedral Road, not far from the entrance to Pontcanna Fields, I find a table, set down my flat white, and take out my notebook, pen, and voice recorder. I'm waiting for Holly Ireland from RBI Wales for a talk about her work with youth baseball. The overall goal of the program, according to the RBI Wales website, is "to create youth leagues in Wales and a training facility in Cardiff so that kids in Wales can have the opportunities to play baseball and softball that children in England have." Through baseball and softball, the program aims to increase participation, social inclusion, and leadership development, while nurturing self-confidence, physical fitness, teamwork, and sportsmanship. Getting these sports to take root, however, is no easy task, as Holly soon explains.

I spot Holly as she walks in the door in her RBI Wales jacket. She smiles and extends her hand before shrugging off her coat and walking to the front to get her own cup of coffee. I notice that underneath her jacket she wears a Padres jersey. She is somewhere in her forties, solidly built, and it's not a surprise that she is a former softball player. In fact, the second thing she tells me is "I came from softball." The first is "Baseball and softball in Wales are not growing as quickly as I'd have hoped, but I'm impatient."

Originally from San Diego—hence the Padres shirt—she moved to Wyoming as a child when her parents divorced. There she played softball, picking it back up again when she moved to Wales in 2006. At that time, there was no baseball team like the Merlins and she had no idea that Welsh baseball even existed. She joined the Cardiff Red Sox, and because she had played before, she quickly became team captain. On the field, they were quite successful, at one time winning a Great Britain Silver Grade National Championship, but eventually Holly's attention turned to the development of a youth program. She says that at the time she was thinking, "The only way this sport is going to grow is if we get the kids in it." In 2016, Holly created South Wales Youth Baseball & Softball, holding an initial event that year. Work commitments interfered in 2017, but in 2018 she returned to the program, trying once again to get things launched. That spring, she was contacted by Ben Kwiatkowski about setting up Little League, and the two of them began to talk about how best to build a youth program. There were three kids there for the first session that summer. The numbers increased over the next couple of years, but then COVID happened and everything had to be re-set.

The approach that RBI Wales has taken has two prongs: the First Pitch program that targets schools, and the baseball and softball groups that Holly runs nearly every night of the week at locations throughout the greater Cardiff area. Schools that sign up for the First Pitch program receive a pack containing a kit and instruction cards for how to use the equipment. Holly also makes herself available to these and other schools for "taster" sessions, a way to quickly introduce kids to baseball and softball. Through the first four months of 2023, she saw approximately two thousand kids across twenty schools. In theory, baseball and/or softball would then make its way into physical education in these schools and perhaps into after-school programs, but in reality, that seldom happens. There is, however, some uptake in evening youth sessions from kids who first see the sport in school, a kind of nascent feeder system that needs to be further developed.

Holly gets about ten or so kids regularly turning up for the sessions that she runs during the week. These kids are broken up into age groups of seven to eleven and twelve and above. While the Thursday fastpitch group—the Celts—now has enough for a team that competes in a league based in Slough, there just aren't yet enough kids on the other nights, especially as baseball and softball have to compete against immensely popular sports like rugby and football for kids' attention. "The only problem," Holly says, speaking of their initial efforts with Little League, "is [that] there isn't anybody to play. We did a lot of training. We tried to play a game in the park once a week, but that can stagnate if you don't have somebody else for them to play. That's the hard thing, and I'm finding it across all the groups." She goes on to say, "That's what all this school work is for—to get the population up so that once we have three teams, we've got fixtures in Cardiff and a season of some sort." Having the population density of Cardiff or Dublin or London is an enormous advantage in getting the critical mass of players needed to establish a youth program. Of course, as I've heard throughout my travels, getting the volunteers needed to coach and organize is perhaps the larger hurdle.

Holly is paid to coach a few hours per week at Howell's School, a private school for girls in the Llandaff neighbourhood of Cardiff, but the vast majority of the work she does in support of youth baseball in Wales is unpaid. Here as elsewhere, the lack of funding for baseball and softball—including funding for youth development—is a major issue, and there is only so much one person can do. As we talk, it's easy to see Holly's passion for youth sport and how important her work is to her. Near the end of our time together, she says, "I love what I do. I love bringing this sport to kids." In the aftermath of our conversation, as I walk towards Sophia Gardens, I can't help but wonder what might be possible if she were paid and could devote herself to this work full time. If there were even a minimal amount of investment in baseball and softball.

SATURDAY, JULY 29, 2023

Saturday morning. No game today, and for the first time since leaving Dundee, I have no work that needs to be done for the project. All this week, interspersed with sessions of notetaking and writing, I had explored parts of the city I hadn't seen on our previous trip here three years ago. I walked west from our flat and into Victoria Park, stopping for coffee at a cafe that overlooked the grass and the trees and the flower beds beyond. I traced the loop from Sophia Gardens up through Pontcanna and Llandaff Fields to the grey stones of Llandaff Cemetery and imposing Gothic facade of Llandaff Cathedral before dropping south for the long walk back to our place just off Cowbridge Road. I strolled the length of Cowbridge, carried along in the wake of its bustle, to Wellington and on across the River Taff. I wandered the beautiful campus of Cardiff University. I drank coffee and took notes at Kin+Ilk and the Pen & Wig and the University Arts & Social Studies Library. I walked the city. Today I will return with Heidi to Cardiff Bay.

We walk south to Lansdowne Road to catch the bus which loops south, past Cardiff City Stadium, before turning southeast through Grangetown on its way across the Taff. We alight at Adelaide, the bay a couple of blocks to our right. But before heading south to the bay, we walk east toward the Wales Millennium Centre, its impressive bronze facade stark against the grey sky. Across its face, in enormous letters, are sayings in both Welsh and English. On the left, the Welsh reads, *CREU GWIR / FEL GWYDR / O FFWRNAIS AWEN*, which in English translates to *Creating Truth Like Glass From Inspiration's Furnace*. On the right, the English says, *IN THESE STONES / HORIZONS / SING*.

We walk south, past the Ferris wheel and the bars and restaurants that line the approach to the quay. We thread our way toward the water, dodging kids running ahead of their parents and couples walking slowly, arm in arm. Across the bay we can see Penarth, and we briefly consider taking the long walk over, past the Norwegian Church and eventually across Penarth Portway. Instead, we push west to the Cardiff Bay Wetlands Reserve with its waterfowl and lily pads and tranquility. Overhead, the clouds hang dark and low, and the wind is a constant, its roar threatening to drown out our conversation.

Despite the wind and the threat of rain, we decide to sit outside for a drink on the water, surveying the silhouettes of sailboats across the horizon. As I sip my beer and gaze across Cardiff Bay, the words arrayed across the Millennium Centre come back to me, transmuted into a message about baseball here that only I can hear. In these stones—these places where makeshift fields go up each week—baseball sings, a song that must continually be nurtured by the stewards of the game I've met on this trip. The truth of baseball in all of these places, created as it is through inspiration and dedication, is like glass, both precious and fragile, but also strong so long as care is taken,

A noise from across the bar pulls me out of my reverie, away from baseball and into the world of my off day. We finish our drinks and make our way towards the exit. The rain holds off, and we begin to walk back to city centre, north along Bute Street, past train tracks on our right and shipping containers converted to housing on our left. Through an underpass, beneath a sign reading *BRAINS BEER*, and into the chaos of city centre on a Saturday afternoon. I raise my jacket hood as a light rain begins to fall.

SUNDAY, JULY 30, 2023

I wake up to a WhatsApp message from Ed: *Sadly today's game is postponed. Forecast is horrible from just before game time and all afternoon!* I have been expecting this decision, but I'm still very disappointed that I won't see a game in Cardiff or be able to talk to anyone else about what baseball here might entail in the future. I had been extremely lucky with the weather through Ireland and Scotland, but in England and Wales, that streak of luck seems to have come to an end. There is no way to delay, no way I can make up the game since tomorrow I will be on a train to Leicester for a week with the Blue Sox and the Diamonds. With teams only playing once a week, the logistics of the trip are, indeed, tricky.

With no game, we try to make the best of it by hopping on a bus to St. Fagans National Museum of History just outside Cardiff. In the time between torrential downpours, we see medieval churches, buildings from sixteenth-, seventeenth-, and eighteenth-century Welsh farms, recreations of nineteenth-century shops, and a workers' institute from early in the twentieth century. As I walk, I think about how the rain had not only washed out the ballgame, but is quickly washing away our visit to this fascinating museum. Past, present, and future all obscured. All I can do now is go home and pack for the last leg of the trip.

LEICESTER

We really wanted to create that safe space for people and do it with baseball at the heart of it.

—ABI "BATTS" BATTISTO,
LEICESTER DIAMONDS

TUESDAY, AUGUST 1, 2023

"How was it to pick up baseball as an adult?"

I'm standing with Suzanne "Suze" Keen at the baseball field shared by the Leicester Diamonds and Leicester Blue Sox that is tucked into one corner of the massive expanse of Western Park on the outskirts of Leicester. Her short blonde hair is tucked under a ball cap that features a drawing of a large blue diamond trailing bright red flames. Dark sunglasses shield her eyes. We're watching the rest of the Diamonds playing catch as Martin Andrews, who everyone simply calls Coach Martin, works his way down the row, working with the players on the mechanics of throwing. "Aim for that target on the chest. Follow through with your arm." Nodding approval at the throw, Martin claps and moves on to the next pair as Suze turns to me and says, "It was fine because everybody started with no knowledge so we're all kind of learning together because it's obviously a very new team."

She joined in 2022 after Martin mentioned to her that he had started coaching the Diamonds: "I came and never looked back. I absolutely love it. I'm probably the oldest one in the team, but I don't let that hold me back." Since then, she has become team captain and part of the seven-person committee that works together to run the team. When I ask her what it is about baseball, she replies, "It's more the team. We've got such a great vibe, such a great team spirit. That's what keeps me coming back." They have approximately thirty-five regular members but are also very accommodating of those who can only attend sporadically, such as young mothers and shift workers. This is just one of the ways the club tries to be as inclusive as possible.

As we talk, a new player in sweatpants, a long brown-and-white striped shirt, and an orange knit cap appears on the sideline. We hear them tell Lizzie "Griff" Griffin that their name is Ray and that they've never played baseball before. Griff smiles and welcomes Ray to the session by first walking them over to a duffel bag filled with gloves that sits behind the backstop before showing them how to wear the glove. The two then walk over to Coach Martin. As the rest of the Diamonds continue to throw, Martin begins to demonstrate to Ray how to throw and catch the baseball. Within minutes, the two are having a catch, Martin occasionally giving advice, but more often simply offering words of encouragement.

Suze and I talk for a few minutes more about the team, their involvement with Leicester Pride as well as local carnivals and fêtes, and their use of social media to spread the word about the Diamonds and their mission. As some of the Diamonds begin to take ground balls on the infield, I comment on how uneven the field is, particularly around third base. Uneven is actually an understatement—it's practically undulating. She acknowledges that the field needs renovation, but says, "At least we've got it—it gets a lot of use." Between the Diamonds and the Blue Sox, there is either training or a game up to four days per week, and so the presence of a functional, if imperfect, field is essential. The backstop is permanent: six full panels—fifteen feet high for the four middle panels and ten feet for the outer panels—that wrap around home plate, extending slightly down each baseline. The diamond itself consists of dirt cutouts for the bases with permanent anchors and a well-maintained pitching mound, while the entire field is ringed almost completely by trees, effectively separating the field from the surrounding geography of Western Park. Little chance here of dog walkers or horses walking across the outfield during a game or training session.

As she walks away to join her teammates, Suze turns back and says, "Batts is the heart and soul of the Diamonds, as far as I'm concerned." Suze and Batts and Griff and the others pair off for the next drill, gloves and balls cast aside. They face each other in a line that stretches toward the outfield, with only a couple of feet in between. About fifteen feet or so behind each line is a pylon. I wonder what they're doing as I see each pair play rock, paper, scissors, the loser turning to sprint for the line behind them while the winner pursues and tries to lay on a tag. There's both intense concentration and a lot of laughter as I watch this odd drill. Eventually, the activity breaks up and Batts comes over to talk. She wears her Diamonds cap backwards over short black hair, glasses, and a white T-shirt embossed with the Diamonds' logo—a baseball diamond superimposed over crossed bats with *LEICESTER DIAMONDS* layered over top. I ask about what I just witnessed, and she tells me that several players wanted a way to work on reactions, agility, and speed, and that rather than falling back on conventional running drills, they instead devised a game that would target the same set of skills. It's clear that an ethic of fun runs throughout everything the Diamonds do.

Abi "Batts" Battisto began playing baseball with the Blue Sox during indoor training in the winter of 2020, becoming hooked within her first few weeks. She loved the training and the experience she was gaining in the development games she was able to play in 2021, when they resumed play after the prior year's lockdown. But, she says, "I knew there was going to be an appetite for this crazy beast that we've created." Batts enlisted the help of Coach Martin (as she always calls him) for this new venture that would become the Diamonds. On that first night in September 2021, they had just five people out, but week by week more players came, some only for a session and others for the long term. The initiative was centred on baseball, yes, but it was ultimately about community, mutual support, and fun. Clearly proud of what they've accomplished in just two years, Batts tells me, "We're [already] the biggest [women's] club in England in the small time we've been together, and you can just see the energy and the love that everyone has for each other. Everyone just wants everyone to do well and, you know, just celebrate each other. So, yeah, it's been really, really good. It's been a wholesome experience so far."

One of the places that the Diamonds have found a large degree of support is the LGBTQIA+ community, and as a club, they have worked hard within BaseballSoftball*UK* (BSUK), Women's Baseball UK (WBUK), and the BBF on issues important to groups often left out of baseball. As Batts puts it, "We've been fighting the fight with the top end of baseball, just trying to get the right policies in place to make sure it is inclusive for all. And we are in a development league, so why would we not make that inclusive?" She goes on to tell me more about their work with Leicester Pride and in the larger LGBTQIA+ community, for which they have been shortlisted by Gaydio for the LGBT+ Club or Sports Team of the Year for the whole of the UK, recognition that she is pleased they are receiving. It's all part of what they call the "Four Cs": Community ("creating our own and celebrating our local community"), Celebrate ("celebrating our members' achievements on and off the field"), Cultivate ("seeking out opportunities to enhance our diamond experience"), and Champion ("advocating for inclusive baseball for all").

I ask why baseball works as a hub for their larger mission, especially within the LGBTQIA+ community. She hesitates, then tells me, "It's actually a bit strange because—I would never want to say this—but *A League of Their Own*..." In almost the same words that Fiona Brambley used when I spoke to her in Slough, Batts tells me about how it being a queer-coded show was an inspiration to a lot of people in the LGBTQIA+ community. Baseball isn't taught in schools here—and they have no expats who played previously, such as Marina DeAngelis in Tayport—so everyone who comes to play with the Diamonds starts at the same level. And since baseball is so little known by most people in the UK, it doesn't carry the baggage or set up the preconceptions that other sports often do. Batts goes on to say, "It's that whole experience of learning something new again. You kind of feel like when you're older, 'Oh, I'm done with all my learning.' To have this fresh sport coming to England is just amazing. None of us have played before, and that's the beauty of it because it's all new and everyone's learning the same things."

I point to Martin and Ray, who are still working together on the mechanics of throwing and catching, and ask about the glove Ray is using. Batts tells me that they were able to buy a lot of basic kit, like the bag of gloves, through a grant from the Sport England's Queen's Platinum Jubilee Activity Fund, monies designated to facilitate sport in depressed areas. Club members have also donated to establish what the Diamonds call the Shine Fund, which covers essential costs such as membership fees and uniforms for players who would not otherwise be able to afford to play. Another expense is equipment, which can be difficult to find in the UK and, when found, is much more expensive than it is in North America. Talking about these initiatives, Batts says, "It just takes away that stigma that you need money to play baseball." It's all part of their efforts at inclusivity and breaking down barriers to participation, whatever they might be. Later Batts will say, "It's not competitiveness; it's just that space where people can come and release. We've got mums; we've got people that work horrendous jobs." The hope is that the Diamonds can be "that space that people come to rely on."

On the field, that translates into a space where players can learn and make mistakes within a supportive environment. Batts describes not only the confidence she has gained as a player—particularly on the mound—but the confidence she has seen growing among her teammates. Much of that can be attributed to Coach Martin and how he calmly teaches the players, but also in the way fun and encouragement weave their way throughout the activities on the field. I can see that now, as Martin gathers the rest of the players on the diamond for a modified game of move-up, with most in the field and four on offence. Players take normal defensive positions, but each "batter" throws the ball rather than hitting. The idea is to work on fielding and on awareness on the basepaths; they'll work on hitting another day. Infielders call out when the ball is in play, helping each other to make the right decision, while after each play Martin gently instructs about where the ball should be thrown in a given situation. There are shouts of encouragement for good plays—grounders successfully fielded, solid throws to first or second base, a pop fly tracked and caught on the run—and much laughter. Later, as training is winding down, the team will do a drill in which Beth "Beef" Cunningham heaves a tennis ball into the air as each Diamond, in turn, tries to trace the arc of the ball and then centre their batting helmet under it, heading it as if it were a football. An unconventional but fun way to practise tracking the path of a fly ball.

We talk a bit about the upcoming visit of the Glasgow Sunflowers, which is scheduled for next weekend. Batts tells me, "We love them. They've got the same kind of ethos as us—you know, it's about fun and that safe space. It's just that community element of it, especially us and them. It's just been phenomenal, and it shows in the numbers."

While the Diamonds are strictly an adult team and will stay eighteen and over so that no one has to filter what they say within the safe space that they have created, the club realizes the importance of youth baseball for the long-term sustainability of the sport. That's why members volunteer their time for First Pitch and Dinky Diamonds, programs designed to introduce baseball to kids and foster an awareness of the sport that was not there when they were growing up. The experience of the Diamonds has shown Batts and others that there is an appetite for baseball in the East Midlands, if not the UK as a whole, but they all understand that sustainability—including youth baseball—is incredibly important. As Batts talks, I hear echoes of earlier conversations, especially when she says, "[It's about] adapting to the environment. Every club is going to be different; every membership is going to want different things, and we've found what our membership wants. If that changes next year, we'll adapt."

I sense that Batts is itching to join the game of move-up so I thank her, ending the conversation so that she can join her teammates. For a few minutes, I sit back on the grass behind home plate, soaking in the late summer sun, marvelling at how much fun this group of people—all new to baseball—is having playing this game. After a few minutes, Beth ("Beef") walks over for a chat. Beef is the team's general manager, "looking after the game-management side of things" such as player development and dealing with the BBF Women's National League. She tells me that there are eight teams in the league, which is divided into two divisions. The Diamonds play each other team in their division home and away, but that leaves a lot of blank spots in the schedule, which they fill in with intrasquad games and friendlies with teams like the Sunflowers. They have enough players to field two teams, but that brings its own challenges, such as how to divide the squad. By skill, with one as competitive and one developmental? Two evenly skilled teams? How does that all fit into the ethos of the club? Some people—including her, I think—would like more competition, while others are focused more on the social element of the club. "It will," she says, "be a question at some point."

I ask how she came to baseball, and she says that it came initially from wanting to move on from competitive field hockey: "I woke up one morning and I just thought, I want to do something new. I could just really hit a ball with a bat. I just had a big urge to do it, and I thought, I don't know if there are any women's baseball teams. At the time, there wasn't—the Diamonds hadn't begun—so I found the Blue Sox." As was the case for Batts, the Blue Sox were not a good fit for Beef, and so she ended up playing slo-pitch for the Leicester Royals, for whom she still plays. Soon after, she saw an Instagram post about the Diamonds forming. She was there at the first training session and has never looked back, telling me, "It's the best thing I've ever done. I was just a member for the first year, and then our GM left and I thought I'd better get involved." I ask her if she can tell me why it's the best thing. She goes quiet for a moment, seems to gather her thoughts before speaking:

> I'm thirty-five. I've been in long-term relationships, and I've never really felt I had a lot of autonomy. Even field hockey I played with my partner. Everything I've every done, I've never really felt like I've done for myself. And this is the first thing I've ever really kind of said, 'This is just for me.' And it was my thing, and I've made the best friends I've ever made in my life. And you've got family. I can't imagine now what my life would look like without this. Without this community.

Learning both the rules and the skills needed in the game has been demanding for all of them, but she thinks that it has helped that they have all come to baseball as adults. Learning to throw, in particular, has been a challenge. As Beef puts it, "We're not a nation of throwers. The little throwing that we do as a kid, we're not taught how to do it properly so we have all this muscle memory about throwing the wrong way." Throws across the diamond from third base and pitching from the same rubber as the Blue Sox have been definite struggles. Despite these challenges, they've been able to acquit themselves well in the games they have played: "We've put up a fight, but we've done it with a smile on our faces. And, you know, I think that actually goes to show that you can take it seriously, play good baseball, but you can have fun."

She thinks there is a real appetite among women to play baseball and that baseball is a sport that suits the community of people who have been marginalized, once they know that it is an option. She says, "It doesn't really matter who you are or [what] your ability [level is]. There is something you can do in this sport. And there are enough roles, even outside of being on the field. We've got some people who say, 'Well, actually, I just like scoring. And I just want to be part of the team.' And they can come along. And we need scorers."

As we talk, both of us have one eye on the game spread out in front of us. A ball takes a wild hop in front of third base, bounding over the head of the fielder and into left field. I shake my head and ask her about the field. She tells me that they would really like to have it rolled, but the Leicester City Council seem to think that there may be something of archaeological significance underneath and so they are not keen on the idea of the teams bringing a steamroller in. After all, Richard III's grave was only recently located under a parking lot in the centre of the city, so I guess they may have a point. Then Beef laughs and says, "Someone told me that part of the beauty of baseball in the States is that every field is different and you have to learn how to play it. This is just our field—full of bumps."

WEDNESDAY, AUGUST 2, 2023

The sky is overcast tonight. There were a few drops as the bus crossed the River Soar, briefly following King Richard's Road before veering on to Glenfield Road. Shops already closed for the night. The famous portrait of King Richard splashed across the shutters of a property agent. Red-brick semi-detached houses. An occasional pedestrian glancing at the sky. A mirror of yesterday's journey. The bus chugs along, ferrying me once again to Western Park, this time for the Leicester Blue Sox training session.

I make my way into the park along a path that will take me past the playground, the place at which I'll turn to walk up a small hill and into the green of the park. It's a long walk across the tall grass before I recognize the place where I need to curve past the stand of trees to emerge in the space where the diamond sits. There are five people there as I approach, and most of them look confused to see me.

I introduce myself and say why I'm here. Still mostly blank stares. Finally, a man wearing a blue-and-green Blue Sox jersey and yellow shorts smiles and says that Matt Crenshaw—my contact with the Blue Sox—did mention that I would be coming to training tonight. He shakes my hand and says his name is Dave Burke, before introducing me to James Arnold, James Brown, Jon Bruce, and Jay Smith. This, he tells me, is the crew for tonight.

As they finish lacing up and stretching out, the five discuss bats and the best place to buy new ones. There's an easy back-and-forth between them, a familiarity bred of their time together over the course of the season. They move to warm-up tosses and then into long toss, arms windmilling between throws as they continue to stretch out. Warmed up, they move to infield practice, each taking a turn hitting ground balls to the others. With only five here, there are plenty of reps for everyone, time to work out where to position the body, how to shuffle the feet, the best arm angle to take in throwing to first. The practice is efficient and useful, and they're clearly enjoying themselves as they put in the work. A different atmosphere and dynamic than last night's Diamonds training. Not better or worse, but very different.

With the transition to batting practice, the players take turns coming over to speak with me, beginning with James Arnold. Bearded, James is dressed in shorts and a Blue Sox T-shirt and cap. He tells me that he started playing baseball in 2001 in Shropshire after watching late-night baseball on Channel 5. He played from the ages of sixteen to twenty-one, but would not play again until 2021, when he picked the game back up at the age of thirty-five. Though he looked up the club when he moved to the area in 2007, life got in the way and he never followed through. It was the pandemic that made him seek out the club again. As James puts it, "I realized I didn't really have a hobby. During COVID, I thought to myself [that] it would be kind of nice to miss something. I wasn't missing anything because I didn't have any hobbies other than work really. So as soon as COVID ended, I hooked back up with the team. And it was really just to establish a hobby. You know, get social again because a lot of that had been missed."

Along with the social aspect, it's the complexity and analytical side that attracts James to baseball. He understands that it is a niche sport in Britain and that, too, is part of the attraction. "You tend to find people of a like mind because they've also got niche interests as well. So they like baseball, being a very niche thing. People of different backgrounds and different walks of life, but baseball is that great uniter of everybody, a common interest that you can share really." He tells me that this small community is like a bubble and that those in the larger community—those not in the know—have no idea that baseball is played in Britain, let alone in Leicester.

I ask whether they normally get more people out to training, and James replies, "This time right now is really the dog days of British baseball. It's when people are on holiday, people have kind of had enough. They haven't liked the results, they're not getting picked, so they tend to stop coming to training or games. As soon as the season starts, everybody's down, kind of thing." He laughs as he finishes talking, clearly amused by the fickleness he's just described. We watch as James B. takes a final cut before taking off his helmet and walking over to trade places with James A.

In the time prior to the start of training, I noticed that James B. was very quiet, listening mostly, interjecting only occasionally. I try to draw him out, ask him about how he got into baseball. He tells me that he started at twenty-one, after seeing people out enjoying themselves playing the game on a sunny day. He's now played for eight years in total, though there have been a few seasons off in between. When I ask what it is that keeps him coming back, he replies, "I think it's just trying to get better. There's a bit of mystique about hitting a baseball. It's trying to hit a ball as far as you can with a bat." Jon Bruce—whose wife also plays baseball, for the Leicester Diamonds—will later tell me something similar when he says, "There's the team aspect, then there's the aspect of—especially in offence—your own skill, kind of doing well for yourself. And then when you're defending, it's doing well for the team kind of thing." James goes on to talk about how much he enjoys being around this group of people. "It doesn't matter, you know, if we're losing, if we're winning; whatever is happening, it's a fun way to spend a Sunday afternoon and a Wednesday evening. Even when it's raining." On cue, the rain begins to lightly fall as Dave calls over to ask the two of us if we want to go to the pub after training. James laughs. "Also, there's always the chance to go to the pub."

After finishing a short bullpen session with Dave, Jay Smith walks over to where I'm sitting. Finished throwing, he's put back on his oversized green hoodie. Like the others, he wears shorts, but also grey tights against the chill of an English summer night. His long curly hair is barely contained by his cap. I ask if we can talk, and he replies with a smile, "It depends if you're a Mets fan or not." I laugh, unzip my jacket to show my Tigers pullover. Jay grew up in South Florida, playing baseball and watching the Marlins, so I understand the joke about the Mets. Preliminaries out of the way, we start to talk.

Jay played baseball from the time he was six until he graduated from high school in 2018. By that time, he was burned out on the game, years of seriously competitive baseball having taken their toll. He moved to Leicester for university in 2020, just as COVID was ramping up, and it was the pandemic that pushed him back to the game. "We were coming out of lockdown, and I was just like, it would be nice to get outside again. I was just curious if there was anything in England, let alone Leicester. And I found the club." I ask how it was getting back into playing after a few years away, and he replies, "For some things, it was sort of like riding a bike. You take so many ground balls in your life—there's a little bit to shake off, but in general that comes back pretty quickly. Seeing live pitching again, that definitely takes some adjusting."

Pitching at this level, he says, is comparable to what he saw playing freshman ball—mid-60s, perhaps a bit of low 70s, with not much off-speed stuff. "Everything is flat. Nothing has really any movement on it. Most teams have one guy who can throw strikes." In terms of his own pitching—a position he's taken up since starting to play here—he messes around with a cutter, slider, and change, in addition to his fastball. Few pitchers in the league have a solid secondary pitch, and hitters aren't used to seeing much outside of a fastball.

Though he played mostly first base in high school, he now plays all over the infield in addition to pitching. Since he has much more experience than most of the players, he's often asked for advice, and players like Jon Bruce point to his influence in helping them to learn the game. Along with Coach Martin, Jay has assisted with coaching the Diamonds, as well. The game does feel different than it did in Florida, especially in terms of intensity and what he calls the "etiquette" of the game. The chatter, for example, is different, muted here compared to what he would hear in South Florida or what I might hear in Southern Ontario or Michigan. But, ultimately, baseball is baseball, and as Jay says, "Everyone out here wants to learn to get better, and that's really all—I think that's what baseball's about and that's all you can really ask for." And that's what I've seen tonight in this extremely efficient session—five people putting in the work and trying to get better.

After training winds down, we make our way to the Forge Inn in Glenfield for a pint and some more conversation. It's a long two-storey building of white-washed brick with a single-storey extension that helps enclose a patio in the back. We get our drinks from the bar and repair to one of the tables on the patio.

The talk drifts almost immediately to the league in which they play—the West Midlands Baseball League. It is a nine-team league, independent of the British Baseball Federation, and has been in existence since 2019, when it broke away from the BBF because of dissatisfaction among clubs with the larger structure. The level is considered to be somewhere between A and AA, and there is a lot of variation in the quality of players within the league and between the league's two divisions, a structure that these players would like to see addressed. What's more, each of these divisions uses different rules, particularly with respect to the use of wood bats, and those differing rule sets have caused problems. Listening to them speak, it's clear that the dissatisfaction with the league has not entirely gone away.

Conversation shifts to the history of baseball in this part of the country, both in Leicestershire and in Birmingham. Baseball, they tell me, has a long history in Birmingham, which is now, at least according to James Arnold, "the second epicentre of baseball" outside of London. Dave adds that the Blue Sox were formed in 2006 "by a guy called Mark Meredith, who played for Birmingham but didn't want to travel over there." There had been a history of baseball in Leicester going back to the '70s and '80s, with baseball being played in the city in Victoria Park by teams like the Green Sox and Dodgers, as well as a couple of others.

"So," continues Dave, "he was able to pick up some ex-players who were in their mid-thirties, early forties, maybe, who had a history of playing." Those players and a few new recruits, along with some Canadians, Americans, and Dominicans who were living in Leicester at the time, formed the first team. Initially, the Blue Sox played in Mountsorrel, a town a few miles north of Leicester, but were asked to leave the field they were using when neighbours complained about what James says were termed "wayward foul balls." Dave joined the team in 2007 after a few years of watching late-night Baseball on Five: "I was watching for four years before I discovered there was British baseball."

We sip our pints and talk about watching baseball on television, about announcers we like and don't like. We talk about the game on Sunday, home against the Birmingham Bats, the more developmental and less experienced of the two teams from the Birmingham club. Beyond our talk, there's little noise on this summer evening, no one else out in the twilight. No one to interrupt what might be the only conversation about baseball in all of Leicestershire tonight.

SATURDAY, AUGUST 5, 2023, A.M.

It's been raining all through the night, a steady patter outside the window of the flat. Today's game, though, is set for Long Eaton, and since I've yet to hear anything about a cancellation, I'm getting ready to meet Martin for a ride in about an hour. As I start to fix breakfast, my phone buzzes. It's a WhatsApp message from Batts telling me that the game is not going ahead. There is, however, a follow-up message: *Martin has said if you still want to meet with him he can meet you for a coffee to have a chat still if you wanted to. Tim Hortons at the clock tower at 8:45?* I quickly agree and ask if any of the players might be up for meeting later in the day.

A half hour later I'm exiting our building, turning right up Charles Street, past Pizza GoGo and the Ale Wagon at the end of our block. I cut left at Halford, over to Gallowtree Gate, shops lining either side of the normally busy pedestrian street. As in all of the city centre, the buildings are densely packed together, the historic interspersed with the more recent, the ornate with the functional. At the end of the block, I can see the brown stone and granite of the Haymarket Memorial Clock Tower. Just to the west is the Tim Hortons, which occupies a striking Tudor-style building, its bright red signs in stark contrast to the painted white brick and ornate black window frames and cornices. It's fair to say that it is wholly unlike any Tim Hortons I've ever seen in Canada. I order a coffee—the first filter coffee I've had in weeks—and move upstairs to wait for Martin to arrive.

Martin Andrews walks over to where I'm taking notes, coffee already in hand, smiling as he sits opposite me. He's in his late fifties, short hair greying under a ball cap wet from the rain that's started again. As he settles in, wiping his fogged glasses on the tail of his shirt, he begins to speak. Martin only started playing baseball in 2016, though he grew up playing football, cricket, and tennis. "I think I was walking past Western Park, because I only live ten minutes away from there, and I saw the baseball going on and I thought, I didn't know we played that over here." He'd seen baseball previously in Canada, on family trips to Toronto, but his exposure was limited. After visiting the Blue Sox Facebook page, he decided to go to bootcamp the following summer. He liked it and got involved. Then something unexpected happened: "I found out that I don't really like the game overly much, the actual game time." He was stuck in the outfield, not seeing enough of the ball, and wanted to be more involved. "But," he says, "I love the drills. So training, I'm there every day, every time it's on—I'm around the corner, to be fair. It's easy. It's reps. I'm all over that like a rash."

During COVID he was the keeper of the kit for the Blue Sox since he lived so close to Western Park, and so he got involved any time someone wanted to train. He enjoyed participating in fielding and batting drills, and he liked thinking up new drills they could use. He started to watch YouTube videos and read books on coaching, and so, by the time Batts approached him about coaching the Diamonds, it seemed to him like something he could do and would enjoy. After agreeing to help with teaching people to throw, catch, and bat, things happened quickly. "The next minute it's rolling. The Diamonds train has started. People coming out of the woodwork everywhere and I'm head coach all of a sudden. And you think, Oh, I don't think I know enough."

But as they began, Jay Smith was able to help out, his knowledge of the game the perfect complement to Martin's ability to teach the basic skills. Jay was, in Martin's words, "a great foil" in that first year.

It's clear from watching the Diamonds training session that the players hold Coach Martin in high regard, but he downplays his role with the team. He tells me, "I do nothing—I don't do the admin, I'm not on the committee, I'm not in their chat. I just organize and turn up for training. If anyone wants extras, I'll do extras. Because I love that." Here he stops, laughs to himself. "I know it's a bit sad. Because a lot of people don't love that, do they? They don't want to do the training; they just want to play. And that's really my backstory and how it is where it is." I ask about the work he did with Ray at training. He becomes animated, speaking with his hands to illustrate his points as he says, "That's what I like, you see. I'm good at that. I think I'm good at that. I don't know if I'm good at that. But to see a lot of them progress—being able to throw this far, struggling, and now they're there and a few of them here, that's good. I get a kick out of that."

Training, he realizes, needs to be fun because not everyone enjoys drills in the same way he does. It's about progress, yes, but also about fun and about the social part of the club, and it's the combination of all these aspects that keep people coming back to training week after week. Some of the activities—like the rock, paper, scissors game and the tennis ball headers game—are player-driven, while others—like the game of move-up played without bats—come from Martin. That game, he says, was a way to create game scenarios, work on communication, and get in throwing reps across the diamond in a simulated game situation. And, just as importantly, a way for the group to have fun while learning to play baseball.

SATURDAY, AUGUST 5, 2023, P.M.

Early afternoon and the rain continues to fall, despite the occasional glimpse of blue sky. As I walk up the high street to The Queen of Bradgate for my meeting with Catherine "Cat" Hawkins and Emma "Dodders" Dodd, I wonder whether tomorrow's game will even be played. No word yet from Dave Burke.

Catherine began playing about eighteen months ago, while Emma has been with the Diamonds since the second training session. Both have been athletes since they were kids—Catherine in team sports, including hockey and football, and Emma in the more individual pursuits of tennis and martial arts—and both see those previous experiences as invaluable in picking up the specific skills of baseball. They discuss, for example, how principles of weight transfer have carried over into learning to hit. Of her experience, Catherine says, "I've really loved learning, because it's such a varied sport. There are so many different elements to it. The people are super encouraging, and it's a big mix of abilities. You know, you don't feel bad coming in and not knowing what you're doing because they're all really welcoming and loads of people don't know what they're doing either." And, she says, "Coach Martin just wants everyone to do better and not just do better, but enjoy it and love it. That's infectious as well." Emma adds, "We've got a bit of a range [of skills], but no one's mean about it. We just all try to help each other. It's not to be sniffed at. It's very important."

I ask them what it is about baseball, and they both first mention the team—the people in the Diamonds, the camaraderie, how much fun they have together, and the level of support they have for each other. Catherine goes on to talk about how much she likes the different challenges presented in baseball: "And you can get it wrong a lot. It's like gambling—especially batting. It's just that one really, really perfect pitch that you hit right is worth the twenty times where you fucked it up." She laughs as she continues, "So I think it's a bit like that. You keep coming back because you're like, I'm going to get that. I'll get it one day. I think that's it—there's always something you can go for next. There's always a specific thing you can strive for."

They tell me how everyone will play different positions, getting a chance to try different things on the baseball field. According to Catherine, chances like those wouldn't be available in other sports such as field hockey or football. But with the Diamonds, it's all part of player development, engagement, and fun. As Catherine tells me, "It's always that vibe. At training, it's never a super-competitive vibe. It's like, let's get the music on, let's celebrate each other." Emma nods, extending the thought: "People are competitive, but they're not competitive in the wrong way."

We talk more about the team, about how they all like to take the piss out of each other. About Batts (Catherine: "Batts's energy is always like that"). About the training session, which Emma says was quite typical, conducted as if I weren't there watching. As we talk, it always comes back to the social aspect of the team and how much they value each other. As Catherine says, "I think it's not just about the sport. I think the sport's, like, important, and we all love it, but..." Emma finishes her sentence, saying, "it's the social side."

Before we leave the pub, Emma stares off into the space at the back of the room. She pauses, looks back to me, and says, "It's nice to be part of it. I think that pretty much sums it up." Catherine nods in agreement and, after a moment, laughs and says, "One day, we'll get that perfect hit or that perfect pitch [and then say] 'Alright, I'm done now. See you.'"

SUNDAY, AUGUST 6, 2023

The phone rings just as I'm starting to prepare for the trek out to Western Park for today's Blue Sox game. The rain stopped last evening, and though there are some dark clouds this morning, there are also hints of blue. I glance at my phone before answering. Dave Burke. This can't be good news.

He says that their field is in bad shape from the rains of the past couple of days—the base cutouts are bogs and home plate is practically under water. Great, I think, another game cancelled. But then Dave continues. "We're moving the game to Marston Green in Birmingham. Playing at midday." Confused, I ask what time in the mid-afternoon as I begin to mentally map out how I might get there. Dave is silent for a second before he speaks. "Midday means twelve p.m. in this country." Glancing at my watch, I tell him that I'll do everything I can to be there. A quick look at the map and the train timetable. Train to Birmingham. Change at New Street Station to the Marston Green stop and then a twenty-minute walk to the park. I'll need to leave in twenty minutes if I have any chance of making it for first pitch.

I drink my coffee and stare at the industrial landscape between Leicester and Birmingham before hustling across the concourse of New Street Station, past the giant statue of Ozzy the Bull that was erected for the 2022 Commonwealth Games, to a commuter platform. Off the second train, I alight at a small suburban station on the outskirts of the city, from which I start walking toward Marston Green. I now find myself on the edge of another enormous city park, wondering yet again how I'm going to find the actual baseball diamond. The cricket pitches are clearly marked on my phone's map, but not the ball field, and right now all I can see are paths leading either along the border between the park and the surrounding suburban neighbourhood, or through vast fields of green grass that seem to have no playing fields at all. It finally dawns on me that the Birmingham Baseball Club may have a more detailed map of the park. The dropped pin leads me to the diamond, just in time for first pitch.

Some of the Bats players are working on the area around home plate as I approach, the Blue Sox congregated around their bench on the third-base side. The mound and dirt areas around the bases are rain slick, muddy, and just barely on the right side of playable. They're putting sand down, spreading it around the plate to try to mop up some of the excess moisture. There is no Quick-Dry here, though sometimes, I am told, they will resort to kitty litter. Anything to get the field into something close to acceptable shape. Getting games in here means a never-ending battle with the weather and occasionally playing in conditions that are less than optimal.

Jay and James Arnold smile and nod as I walk up to the bench. Dave, Jon, and the other James—who I'll learn today they call JB—are there as well. Dave introduces me to some of the other players—Rikson Martina, Kenshin Akahori, Neil Davies. Since the game has been shifted from Western Park, the Blue Sox will be the home team today, and so they are all waiting to take the field once the repairs to it are complete. Starting today for the Blue Sox will be Said Bayan, a young player somehow affiliated or previously affiliated with Birmingham. It's unclear to me whether he has moved closer to Leicester and is now, in fact, playing for the Blue Sox. Whatever the reason, he is pitching.

The game opens with a walk, two steals, and an overthrow to plate the first run. A strikeout swinging, but then another walk and an immediate steal of second. Rik, who's been cajoled into keeping score until he comes into the ballgame, shakes his head and makes notations to record what's happened. Bayan seems to settle himself and starts to throw strikes again, getting the next two batters to strike out looking. Rik notes the Ks as he turns to me and says, "Once you see a diamond, you get excited." His teammates run off the field, cheering each other on to score some runs.

They start off with two quick outs—a pop-up to the pitcher and a strikeout—before Jay manages to get aboard when the second baseman can't handle a sharply hit ground ball. After Daniel Goodman walks, James A. singles to cash in both runs before scoring himself on a wild pitch. Though there are shouts of encouragement as the walks, steals, and hits add up to a lead, the atmosphere remains serious, a playoff spot riding on the results of their last few games. By the time they take the field again, the Blue Sox have the lead, the score 3–1 in their favour. I lean back on my stool and begin to talk to Rik as the young pitcher takes his warmup tosses.

Rik tells me that he grew up in the Caribbean and started playing baseball there when he was eight years old. At twelve, he moved to the Netherlands and resumed playing baseball at fourteen, playing continuously for the next seven years. After moving to England, he started up again at the age of twenty-six. He's been with the Blue Sox for four seasons, mostly pitching and playing centre field these days, though he will also catch and play shortstop. The league is certainly below the level of competition at which Rik has played in the past, and it shows in his statistics—he will finish the year with a batting average of .479 and an OPS of 1.212. In 2018, he played in the National Baseball League, the highest level in British baseball, with a team based in Birmingham but with players from all over the country. Though they had a lot of experienced players, they didn't have enough time to prepare and did not do well in the league. They lasted only a year. From there he moved to the Blue Sox.

I ask him what it's like playing baseball in Britain. He leans back on the overturned bucket that serves as his stool and says,

> It's better organized in the Netherlands, from my personal experience, compared to here, but at the same time, we do have a lot of competitive teams. Just a diversity of players, where you might have five experienced and then the rest of the squad probably first year, second year. So, you are finding a lot of teams that you probably encounter, probably three or four players supporting the whole team throughout the season.

He goes on to tell me that another difference is that in the Netherlands, you would be benched for missing training and that your performance in the training sessions determined playing time. Nothing like that would ever happen in Britain, where the onus instead must be on player development at a more basic level. Being one of the more experienced players on the team, he enjoys the challenge of trying to bring newer players up to speed: "For me personally, you have to put your ego aside. You're only as good as your weakest player. So, if you don't support your lowest players, who would, say, have less experience, and bring them up to your level or to the team's level, shall I say, you know you're going to struggle to be competitive in an actually competitive league." In a fight for first place with the Birmingham

Metalheads in West Midlands Baseball League's Eastern Division, the Blue Sox seem to have been able to bring their less experienced players up to a competitive level.

We watch as Bayan continues to alternate between walks and strikeouts. He has yet to give up a hit, but the walks combined with untimely errors have yielded a second run for the Bats. In listening to Rik talk, I sense that there's something he's not yet said about playing baseball in Britain as opposed to the Netherlands. As another walked batter trots to first, he leans towards me and says, "The politics would make you not want to play if you didn't have the heart for it." While the next batter settles into the box, rain begins to fall. A grin breaks out face on Rik's face. "At the end of the day, as long as you've got a bit of heart for the sport, which we all do, you know, you enjoy coming out on a Sunday, even when it's raining, to play a bit of baseball." His deep laugh echoes across the park as Said records his sixth strikeout of the game for the final out of the inning.

There is subdued cheering from the Blue Sox bench as they begin their half of the second inning, up 3–2. Fresh off two innings on the mound, Said comes to the plate with one out and beats out an infield single before Jon singles to put two men on base. Jay is coming in to pitch next inning, and to my left, I can hear him talking to Neil about the signs to use. Jay has five pitches—two-seam, four-seam, slider, curve, and change—so they'll need more than Neil just putting one or two fingers down. It's Jay's final season with the Sox, and it's clear he wants to pitch as much as he can before he returns to the US. As they talk, Dave hits a sacrifice fly to make the score 4–2. It will be 6–2 by the time Jay takes the mound. Rik predicts a walk and two strikeouts for Jay this inning, and he's not far off, as Jay gets a groundout to the pitcher and two strikeouts sandwiched around a single on a swinging bunt.

With a 6–2 lead, the Blue Sox bench is starting to loosen up. Jay and Rik discuss how people approach different levels of competition, whether they can maintain concentration when the other team isn't as good, when it's a team they should beat easily. I get snatches of a story about Neil umping a Blue Sox game and calling an out on the Sox when Dave caught a foul ball when he was coaching third base. "Let's go, JB." Someone starts singing "Get on Up," walk-up music that only a few of us can hear. Jay and Rik have moved on to a discussion of the difference between the kind of swings you take at the plate and the outcome of those swings. The line drives that are hit straight at a fielder, the bloop singles that fall into the perfect spot.

Jay takes the mound for a second inning of work with the score 7–2 Blue Sox. I walk over to Kenshin, who all the Blue Sox call Kenny, and ask if we can talk. He's originally from Japan and has been playing baseball since he was six years old. As an infielder in Japan, he played at a very high level, especially when he was in junior high. He says, "Japanese baseball is high intensity. I played under tons of pressure." Coaches would focus on mistakes—not just errors—but communication mistakes, mistakes in body positioning, and even small mistakes in both games and in training would mean that you didn't play. When he was in junior high, he wanted to go to the national competition, but when he realized he was not talented enough to do so, he left the stress behind and opted to play at a less competitive level for high school. As Kenshin puts it, "I wanted to have fun in baseball—I realized that. I chose having fun, not playing competitive."

He moved to Leicester two years ago to pursue a Business Entrepreneurship and Innovation degree at De Montfort University. I ask about what it was like to move from

Japan to the middle of the UK, and he replies, "It was very hard to find a common hobby and common interests in England. Because I'm from Japan, I spent most of my time on baseball. But, you know, England doesn't have baseball culture." On the off chance, though, he googled *baseball in Leicester* and found the Blue Sox, and he's now been with them for two years. He feels at home with the team: "We obviously have a common hobby. When we can have a conversation—MLB, Japanese League, you know. I really have fun talking about the Japanese League in England because some people are really interested." We watch a fly ball arc and land in the glove of the left fielder for the third out of the inning. The team returns from the field, squeezing under the tarp that's been erected to protect the players from the rain. Kenshin turns to me and says, "The time I [first] came here, I couldn't speak English, to be honest." Neil stops taking off his shin guards, a very surprised look on his face as he says, "Really!?" Kenshin continues, "I had lots of hesitation, just when I speak English, but they are lovely. You know, they have the same hobby or topic of conversation. Even if I don't know some words, I can communicate. So that's why I can feel like home. Today I'm not playing for the team. I still have fun."

Over the next two innings, the Blue Sox will score ten more runs, the mercy rule invoked after five innings with the score 17–2. Neil will steal a base, and one of his teammates will yell, "Neil with a stolen base. Somebody call the cops!" Rik will play shortstop for an inning. The Blue Sox will turn a nice 6–3 double play. The sun will come out. Kenshin will come up to bat, his teammates chanting "Kenny! Kenny!" Neil will throw only submarine pitches as he comes in to pitch to one batter. The game will officially end, but with the sun out, the teams will keep playing for a couple more innings. Rik will pitch for the Bats against his own team. Jon will pitch for the Sox. There will be banter. There will be much laughter. Even though it ends in a mercy, it will be a good day out.

As everyone begins to pack up, I sit down for a chat with Neil. He started playing when he was fourteen years old, in the U16 Pony League in Nottingham. He and his best friend were inspired by watching Baseball on Five, first getting ahold of a couple of gloves so they could play catch all winter and then finding a team the next spring. It was baseball until he aged out of Pony League, but then his attention shifted to fastpitch. "Baseball took a backseat just because it wasn't around, but it would have been my preferred version." He played for fifteen years on the Great Britain men's fastpitch team, a team that was one of the best in the world because of the fact that it was able to draw excellent players from all over the Commonwealth. As Neil says, "Because it's more of a niche sport, there were more opportunities." He's played with a few local teams over the past few years and just joined the Blue Sox halfway through last season "when the Nottingham team was falling apart."

Jay interrupts, saying to Neil, "How was my catching, coach?"

"You should have had an out at third. Now you can feel my pain. You make the play and there's no one there to make the tag."

Jay laughs, goes back to unlacing his cleats. I ask Neil what it is about baseball that attracts him. He replies:

> The mental. I love the situational stuff. I love catching because you're pulling strings. Maybe not in a game like this, but when you're at a high level and you have to think three steps ahead of

> the hitter. He's sitting on this because we've just thrown him this and last at bat we got him with that. I love all that stuff. I think when I'm not able to catch any more, I don't know if I'll want to play. I don't want to just stand out there and throw a ball every now and then. I like being in that field general type of role. Maybe manage rather than...

His voice trails off. Perhaps he's thinking about that point in the future where he can no longer play, that time when he can no longer crouch behind the dish, no longer take the wear and tear on his knees and his already bad shoulder.

Before we follow the others to the pub, I ask how it's been to play for the Blue Sox. He perks up and says, "Great. British baseball has a lot of politics. It has a lot of people with strong opinions on how their own team should be run, how their league should be run. But this has been one of the most calm teams to play for, if that's the right way to say it. There's been very little controversy. It's been really good coming here." We both start to rise as Dave yells for everyone to meet at The Little Owl for a pint before we all head back to Leicester.

We sit on the patio with our drinks, enjoying the sun on our arms after a day of rain. We talk mainly of baseball, here in Britain, but also in the major leagues. I listen as they discuss the push for the upcoming playoffs, dissecting their remaining games and who might make the playoffs from each division. They talk about pitching in the league, about the overall tendency in British baseball to give pitchers too long a leash before taking them out because most teams have so little pitching depth. I look around the tables.

James. JB. Dave. Jon. Jay. Kenshin. Danny. Rik. Neil. The Blue Sox. The final team of my summer of chasing baseball.

I pile into JB's car with Jay and Kenny, waving goodbye to the other players. There's an easy camaraderie in the car between the three of them. They talk about Jay's move to New York and whether he still has eligibility left to play for Lehman College. About where Kenny will get an internship for his program. About how JB's job is going. And, of course, they talk about baseball, this unlikely group of friends—one from the US, one from Japan, and one from England—drawn together by their shared passion for the game. I think of all the parks I've seen, all players with whom I've talked, all the good days out I've had watching baseball this summer. Someone asks what I'm thinking about, and I smile and reply, "Baseball."

EPILOGUE

> You can learn to play baseball in a day,
> but you'll be mastering it for a lifetime.
>
> —JASON WEST, TAYPORT BREAKERS

When I first conceived the idea of *Makeshift Fields*, I was driven by little more than curiosity, by the novelty of there being baseball in Ireland, Scotland, England, and Wales. The chance to see the game I love in places both familiar and new—to spend another summer chasing baseball—was enticing in and of itself. But as I spent time with and talked to players, coaches, parents, scorekeepers, umpires, and spectators in these locales, the project came to be much more. I began to feel a deep responsibility to show what baseball means to all of these people. A deep responsibility to get it right.

This book is a snapshot of grassroots baseball, an exposure of one summer. In the seven weeks I spent immersing myself in the game as it is played in these places—in the rain and cold, with temporary diamonds on makeshift fields that are sometimes less than ideal—I came to respect the fragility of what's been created and the enormous group effort that's needed to sustain it. I came to see this as the story of people who love the game, the story of people who believe that baseball can flourish in Dublin and Cork. In Aberdeen and Edinburgh and Tayport. In Cardiff. In Leicester and London and Essex and Norwich and Slough.

On one hand, baseball is baseball, and what I saw—despite some idiosyncratic rules and an incredibly wide range of talent and experience—is not dissimilar to what I might see on any given night in Windsor, Ontario. On the other hand, it feels different. More precarious, yes, but also more communal. What I saw is Irish baseball. Scottish baseball. English baseball. Welsh baseball. It's baseball that is growing where it's been planted, developing according to the idiosyncrasies of each location. There are, of course, differences across these teams and across these regions, but what they have in common is an emphasis on baseball as a site for both community and fun, with improvement and competition woven into, rather than superseding, these central facets of the game as it is played in these places. In all but a very few cases, there is no next level, no other team to which players can aspire. There is instead baseball for its own sake, played in public parks by people who have somehow fallen in love with the game or are searching for a piece of home.

As so many people told me, you have to love baseball to play it in Ireland or Scotland or England or Wales. Chasing baseball to all of these places reaffirmed for me why it is I love this game.

ACKNOWLEDGEMENTS

I would first like to thank all the players, coaches, umpires, parents, spectators, and volunteers who spoke to me over the course of the summer I spent chasing baseball so far away from my home. Those conversations were invaluable to me in understanding baseball in all the places I visited, the myriad reasons that it is important to everyone involved, and the long list of challenges baseball faces as a niche sport in these countries. Without those interactions and conversations, there would be no *Makeshift Fields*.

Among the people I met that summer, I need to single out a few people for special thanks: Jason Wiebe and Sean Mitchell (Baseball Ireland and the Ashbourne Giants), John Dillon (Red Rox), Leo Farrell and Daniel Woodburne (Mariners Baseball Ireland), Brett Sutherland and Andrés Fornes (Cork Renegades), Casey Mackenzie (Aberdeen Oilers), Sylvain Morisot (Edinburgh Diamond Devils), Jason West and Liam Quinn (Tayport Breakers), Ed Peebles (Cardiff Merlins), Abi "Batts" Battisto and Martin Andrews (Leicester Diamonds), and Dave Burke (Leicester Blue Sox). You all have no idea how much I appreciate the welcome you gave me and all of the help you provided before, during, and after the trip.

At Invisible Publishing, I need to first and foremost thank Norm Nehmetallah. I came to Norm late in the summer of 2022 with the somewhat bizarre idea about travelling around Ireland, Scotland, England, and Wales in search of baseball. He was enthusiastic from the jump, and I can't thank him enough for his support and for the work he did in editing the book.

I must also thank a couple of other important people at Invisible. First, a big thanks to Megan Fildes for the striking cover design and the beautiful interior design of the book. As well, I am incredibly grateful to Kimberley Griffiths, Director of Editorial and Production, for giving me the most detailed and thorough read I have ever had at the stage of correcting proofs. This book is immensely improved through her efforts.

Finally, I would like to thank the University of Windsor for their support in the research and writing of this book.

Invisible Publishing produces fine Canadian literature for those who enjoy such things. As an independent, not-for-profit publisher, we work to build communities that sustain and encourage engaging, literary, and current writing.

Invisible Publishing has been in operation for nearly two decades. We released our first fiction titles in the spring of 2007, and our catalogue has come to include works of graphic fiction and nonfiction, pop culture biographies, experimental poetry, and prose.

We are committed to publishing writers with diverse perspectives. In acknowledging historical and systemic barriers, and the limits of our existing catalogue, we emphatically encourage writers from LGBTQ2SIA+ communities, Indigenous writers, and writers of colour to submit their work.

Invisible Publishing is also home to the Bibliophonic series of music books and the Throwback series of CanLit reissues.